THE GUNSHIP CHRONICLES

by

Larry D. Barbee

DEDICATION

1972- 1973

A good story should have a beginning, a middle, and an end. Most persons who write stories about their time in Vietnam have, instead, a start, a middle, and a stop. Their character was on the stage for only a brief period between the opening and closing scenes of the conflict. They missed the beginning and left before the end. The only ones who had an end were those who did not come home.

If I have earned the right to dedicate a book about Vietnam to someone, it would be to Terry Courtney, who met his end, so that I and others could stop, and return.

ACKNOWLEDGEMENTS

Thanks to Roy Davis for the idea of putting this story out there, for encouragement, and especially for technical support and knowledge of the on-line publishing and printing process.

Thanks to my beautiful wife Debbie for 49 years of tolerance. Every time I came home and told her I wanted to fly an airplane that flew in circles at low altitude over enemy positions, or I wanted to fly one that flew faster than a bullet at 200 feet above the ground at night in the mountains, she always said: "Well, just increase your insurance."

Recently I thanked her for her support and patience for all these years. I told her that if she kept up the good work, I'd put her in my book.

Thanks to my friend Walt, who helped me understand and adapt to my first operational assignment.

And a very big thanks to whoever packed my parachute.

PROLOGUE

The Air Force called them fixed-wing gunships, in order to differentiate them from the Army's helicopter gunships. The gunship crews called them Spooky, Shadow, Stinger and Spectre, depending on which particular aircraft type they flew.

The Viet Cong called them dragonships, because dragons were symbolic and they respected the tremendous rain of fire gunships brought down on their positions. American aircrews did their best to convince them the aircraft did indeed have dragon like powers and gunships came to be called Puff, after the ballad of Puff, the Magic Dragon.

The gunships were a successful experiment in which cargo aircraft were converted to attack aircraft. They were ungainly and much slower than the more glamorous jets, but they could loiter for hours in search of targets or in defense of troops on the ground. They carried advanced sensor systems and immense firepower to rip away the nighttime blackness that protected the enemy.

Gunship crews roamed the night over Laos, Cambodia and South Vietnam. The missions were exotic, exciting and dangerous. And when the missions supported American troops on the ground, they were very, very satisfying.

GLOSSARY

AAA	Anti-Aircraft Artillery - Cannon or machine guns used to defend against enemy aircraft
ARC LIGHT	ARC LIGHT B-52 Bombing raid against targets in South Vietnam, Laos or Cambodia.
ARVN	South Vietnamese Army.
BDA	Bomb (or Battle) Damage Assessment.
BINGO	Aircraft fuel state where aircraft must depart its target area to have sufficient fuel to recover at its intended landing base.
DMZ	Demilitarized zone between North and South Vietnam.
FAC	Forward Air Controller
FOL	Forward Operating Location.
FLIR	Forward Looking Infra-Red.
KBA	Killed By Air.
KIA	Killed In Action.
LAW	Light Anti-tank Weapon.
MIG	Soviet built (or produced on contract by other nations) jet fighter aircraft.
NOS	Night Observation Sight.
NVA	North Vietnamese Army.
SAM	Surface to Air Missile.
STRELLA	Shoulder launched infra-red homing missile used by North Vietnamese forces.
TIC	Troops in Contact

OVER LAOS

Cash McCall leaned over my shoulder and squinted out the open gunship door at the Laotian jungle beneath our wing. The moon textured the tall trees with dusty gray shadows and silvered each stream winding through the dense growth below. It was well after midnight and the world seemed deserted. There were no signs of life, no villages, no roads, no fires. Major McCall's face was creased in a frown visible even in the darkened cargo compartment.

I knew that any people on the ground below our airplane would do their best to remain invisible. In this part of Laos, any vehicle was a target and the drivers travelled with as much stealth as possible. Headlights could bring fire and death. The Ho Chi Minh Trail was the nightly hunting ground for US Air Force gunships flying from Thailand and South Vietnam. It was no place to attract attention or take chances. The gunships' primary goal was slowing the flow of North Vietnamese supplies and troops being trucked south to support the Viet Cong and North Vietnamese army.

The aircraft were equipped with special sensors to help the crews detect this traffic. As a Night Observation Sight, or NOS, operator aboard AC-119K gunships, my duties would be to use a device that amplified the available light from the moon, stars or flares to find targets on the ground. In gunship dialect, both the sensor and the operator were called NOS, pronounced as one would pronounce the first half of nostril.

When a target was positioned in the NOS crosshairs, the target location was passed electronically to our fire control computer which allowed us, when the myriad switches were correctly set and triggers depressed, to fire two 20 millimeter cannon and four 7.62 millimeter miniguns at the selected target.

The NOS performed this operation while standing in an open door in the left side of the aircraft cargo compartment, just aft of the cockpit. The sight was positioned above a small, vertically mounted square of ceramic armor that protected the operator's legs up to mid-thigh and helped keep him from falling out when the aircraft maneuvered to avoid anti-aircraft fire.

Another small piece of this armor was secured to the aircraft floor for the NOS to stand on. It was supposed to stop small caliber bullets or shrapnel coming up through the bottom of the airplane. Beside the NOS, toward the rear of the aircraft, were the six guns. The machine guns or miniguns were used against troops in the open and the twenty millimeters were effective against trucks, troops and watercraft.

Since our guns were mounted in the left side of the aircraft, our tactics were restricted to going into a circular orbit around the target, banking the plane to point the guns toward the ground and shooting where the sensors were aiming.

An advantage of this arrangement was that on a relatively calm night when winds were low, we could shoot at the target from all around the circle. An obvious disadvantage was that we were going in circles, at slow speed and low altitude, around a target that might shoot back. The effect was much like that of Redskins circling a wagon train in a John Wayne movie. Since the Indians frequently got the worst of this maneuver, we preferred to fly at night, where our sensors allowed us to see the enemy positions and they usually could not track us.

For the pilots, however, even the practice of night fighting could be disconcerting. Unlike the sensor operators, the pilots usually could not see the target in the darkness, but they could see the anti-aircraft fire directed back at us. One pilot described it as staring into a black bucket held at arm's length and watching roman candle balls come out the bottom.

Tonight, however, we would not be targeting vehicles on the trail. We were headed North at our maximum speed to support a friendly outpost expecting attack by Pathet Lao or North Vietnamese army units. The change of mission had come after takeoff and we had few details on the situation.

It was this sudden change in plans that had Major McCall worried. He was along to evaluate my performance and to clear me to fly combat missions as a combat ready crewmember without an instructor.

This mission was my third flight in Southeast Asia and was supposed to be my final check-out flight.

Truck hunting along the trail had been the objective. Instead, this mission would be my first exposure to a "Troops in Contact" or "TIC" situation. We had never trained to support troops in close combat in our stateside checkout program.

The Major was not supposed to give me any help or advice on my check ride, but when troops were closely engaged with the enemy, accuracy, speed and clear communications were vital for close air support. With our cannon and miniguns, a mistake could instantly wipe out the people we were trying to save. The important thing now was to get to our friends on the ground and put down fire support. The check ride was secondary to the mission, and Major McCall had to decide whether to take over or let me continue the check. I badly wanted to play my part in any fighting and Major McCall must have sensed my eagerness. He decided to give me a chance to handle the situation.

"Okay, Larry, you got the mission, unless you start to foul it up. This is going to be your on the job training for troops in contact. I know this isn't what we planned for, but this is the real world and your missions will change all the time over here.

"Now, when we get there, be prepared for all kinds of shit over the radios. Everybody will be hollering. This guy will be Laotian or at least pretending to be, so he'll have an accent and if he's excited you may not be able to understand him. Just take your time and make sure you've got the right target before we shoot. We want to kill the bad guys, not the friendlies."

In the dark, I nodded to show I understood.

He continued, "When we start working the TIC, there may be tracers and flares and mortar impacts all over the place. The bad guys probably know Bald Head's radio frequencies and listen in. They may try to break in to jam or spoof us. Just keep your cool and work with the rest of the crew. Never be afraid to speak up when something doesn't look right, cause I'll guaran-damn-tee you things won't look right sometime during the night.

We already knew the radio call sign for the Laotian Forward Air Guide, or FAG, who was on the ground at the outpost. "Cricket," the Airborne Command and Control ship, who had diverted us, had passed us all the details they had. When we reached the approximate area of the outpost, we were to contact "Bald Head" on one of our FM radios. Bald Head and other FAGs were Laotian soldiers who had received special training to help lead their countrymen against the communists, either foreign or home grown. Part of their training dealt with working friendly air support against enemy positions.

Tonight, as always, we would contact him using our permanent squadron call sign of "Stinger." On the radio, we would be "Stinger 31" and he was simply called Bald Head.

The airborne battle staff aboard "Cricket" would also eavesdrop on as much of the radio chatter as it could and would not hesitate to put an oar into our business. When everyone was shouting on the radio at the same time, the noise could blanket important transmissions and create maddening confusion. Fortunately, at my position, I could selectively cut out radios and monitor only the ones I considered the highest priority.

Rich Hanson, as our crew "Table Navigator," had the responsibility of coordinating our attack with the ground FAG. He controlled the attack and our fire control computer, made sure we had clearance to fire and that we put the bullets on the right target. He would be the primary communicator between Bald Head and our aircrew.

As we neared the coordinates of the outpost, patchy low clouds covered much of the ground below us. No lights were visible in the murky jungle. Looking through the NOS, I saw no evidence that humans had ever set foot in the jungle below. We rolled into an orbit at an altitude that put us between the growing cloud cover and the many limestone peaks, called karsts, which rose from the jungle like dragons' teeth.

Rich made the first call for our FAG. "Bald Head, Bald Head, Stinger 31."

Immediately, a solemn voice with a thick oriental accent came back on the radio, "Roger, Stinger. This Bald Head. You come work with Bald Head?"

"That's affirmative, Bald Head. What is your situation?" "Stinger, this Bald Head. You say again, please?" Rich tried again, simplifying the words in his transmission and speaking more slowly. "Bald Head, this is Stinger. How can we help you?"

"AAh, Stinger, we have many bad guys all round. Can you give flare and maybe shooty-shoot. Some maybe one hundred meters from my position. They no do big attack yet..."

I shook my head and looked at my interphone panel to see if the switches were correctly set. Did I really hear Shooty-shoot? I wouldn't have believed someone would rely on baby talk just before the start of a firefight.

Rich, however, had heard it all before. "Bald Head, Stinger. Chai, Cop, we shooty-shoot and you checky-check."

"Chai, Cop" was the Thai equivalent of "Yes, sir or Yes, Mister."

Then, using codes, Rich verified that we were in contact with the real Bald Head and not an imposter.

Enemy spoofing with friendly radio call signs was not unheard of in Laos.

I was beginning to understand what Major McCall meant when he warned me about unusual radio procedures. Oh, well, I thought. Whatever works. Like the rest of the crew, I was ready to get down to business. The first step was to find Bald Head and get a good fix on his position. With the weather thickening, we needed to take care of his problem before the clouds clamped down and left the enemy free to maneuver without worry of air attack.

Rich began the location attempt. "Bald Head, Stinger. Can you give me a long count on your VHF radio? I want to find your position."

"Stinger, this Bald Head. Roger, I give you long count now. One, two, three, ... "Bald Head continued the count up to ten and then backward down to one. He was transmitting on both FM and VHF (very high frequency) radios, a technique known as simulcasting. In the navigator position, Rich's radio compass needle pointed the direction toward Bald Head's radio. Rich checked the chart for high terrain along a line from our present orbit to Bald Head's radio transmitter.

"Pilot, Nav. The radio steer checks out with Bald Head's reported position. Let's come around to two nine zero and go down to fifty-eight hundred feet pressure altitude. That will put us at 'Charlie' altitude for this area. Nearest high terrain is three miles south, a big karst at four thousand feet."

"Coming right to two nine zero degrees," the pilot responded. I'll start descent when we're on heading. Crew, pilot. Everybody on your toes, we're heading in. Engineer, back me up on altitude."

Shortly after we "crossed the fence" into Laos from Thailand, we had completed most of the checklists that insured we were ready for firing. Only a few details of internal coordination remained before we were ready to go to work in earnest. Rich took care of some of them, crosschecking the altimeter settings in the cockpit and briefing the rest of the crew on the nearest suitable bailout and safe areas in case we should be hit and forced to use our parachutes.

The pilot rolled out on heading and eased the throttles back. The engines slowed and the plane nosed over in a gentle descent that took us through a thin layer of cloud. The throttles came forward again and the pilot called level at 5,800 feet.

Now we were under a thin but complete overcast and in a not very desirable situation. The moonlight spreading over the top of the cloud layer created a backlight effect that outlined our plane as a moving shadow. We had lost the cover of night and were now exposed to any gunner who wanted to take a shot at us. We had no choice. We had to be able to see the target to work. It seemed likely that the weather would drive us down even further before the mission was completed.

"Bald Head, Stinger 31. We are inbound to your position now. Do you have a strobe light to signal us when we pass over you? Over.”

"Stinger, this Bald Head. We no have strobe light."

"Okay, Bald Head, we do it another way. We fly over you. You call us when we over your position. Do you copy, Bald Head?"

"Roger, Stinger. Bald Head copy."

As we droned toward the FAG's outpost, I scanned as far forward as possible with the NOS to find anything to indicate his location. There was nothing but dense jungle. The reduced moonlight below the cloud level cut down on the available illumination that made the instrument work. Inside the eyepiece, the world was only a round green image of trees. With only a single eyepiece, there was little depth of field and all objects in the viewer appeared flat and two-dimensional. When I stepped back from the NOS, the combination of green afterimage on the retina of my right eye and the solid black night outside the NOS door brought an uncomfortable sensation of vertigo.

Bald Head's eager voice came through my helmet earphones. "Stinger, I hear you now. You coming right to me. You over me, NOW!"

Rich spoke rapidly, "Pilot, Nav. Take up a left orbit. We're clear of high terrain at this altitude for several miles."

"Bald Head, Stinger," Rich called. "We go into orbit now. Now we look for you. When we find you, you tell us where bad guys are."

"Roger, Stinger. Bald Head copy."

"NOS, Nav. Can you see anything of his position? He should be out there about Dead Nuts. Look for some kind of fire base or bunker complex. Could be a walled in village."

Dead Nuts was a term used to indicate a position on the ground directly in the center of the orbit. It was a good reference point

13

from which to start a search or to use as a base reference when describing a target location for another sensor operator.

I swept the NOS scope through Dead Nuts and all areas of the orbit, but the inhabited area I expected to see just wasn't there. Instead I saw a shimmering screen of tracer bullets burst from the edge of a small opening in the jungle to skip and ricochet from what appeared to be a bare patch on a hillside.

Suddenly the fire shifted up, drawing a green line that rose toward us and then arced away and down. The bullets seemed to float slowly until they neared us, but when they went beneath, they were moving like hell.

Somebody down there didn't like us and was showing it with automatic small arms fire. There was not much chance of the gunner hitting a moving target at our altitude and range, but either he didn't know that or he didn't care. Through the NOS, the string of tracers looked like water streaming from a garden hose at full pressure.

As I moved the NOS to cover the source of the fire, I felt a hand on my shoulder and Major McCall said, "Leave him alone for now. We have to know where the friendlies are before we shoot. If he gets to be a nuisance later, we'll grease him."

I was a little chagrined that the major had felt it necessary to remind me of our priorities, but I understood. We first had to locate Bald Head and work from there. He would be able to point out the enemy positions that were giving him the most trouble. If we just hosed lead around, we weren't guaranteed of hitting the bad guys and just might hit our friends. The major didn't need to remind me what would happen if we fired on friendly positions.

I keyed the interphone mike and said, "Nav, NOS, I don't see anything that looks like a built-up area. The light's pretty dim

14

under these clouds. But that machinegun could be firing at Bald Head. The tracers are hitting a bare area up a hillside."

"NOS, what color are those tracers?"

"Nav, NOS, they're green."

"Okay, NOS. Usually the bad guys shoot green small arms and machinegun tracers and the good guys use red. But you can't be sure because the bad guys will use anything they can capture and may use red too. Keep an eye on where those green tracers are hitting and see if you can see anything on the ground when I talk to Bald Head."

"Bald Head, Bald Head, Stinger 31. We see green tracer bullets hit hill. Are those bad guys shooting at you?" "Stinger, this Bald Head. Bad guys shoot at me and you too. You see my position?" Bald Head pronounced the word position with a very long "oh" sound, "poosition".

"Bald Head, we think we see your poosition on hill. Are you on side of hill where green tracers hit?" Rich was unconsciously duplicating Bald Head's accent and delivery.

"Stinger, this Bald Head. We on side of hill. Bad guys shoot pretty close. You see us now?" "Bad guy, I mean Bald Head, this Stinger 31. We think we see where you are. You want to shoot flare? We watch and see where flare come from. When we sure it's you, we go to work, Chi?"

"Stinger, Bald Head. Me shoot flare. Stand by."

"NOS, Nav, stand by and see where the flare comes from and lock on that position."

"Roger, Nav." Green tracer bullets still reached out to peck at the hillside. I was sure the flare would come from there.

"Stinger, Bald Head. Me shoot flare now."

15

I glued one eye to the NOS eyepiece and kept it pointed at the bare patch on the slope. I kept the other eye open to try to watch out for the flare if it came from somewhere else. ~-

A tiny puff of light burst from the area that had spawned the machine gun tracers. Almost simultaneously, small bright ground flashes came from two other quadrants. Seconds later three mortar flares burst into brilliant light and began their shimmering descent beneath swinging parachutes. All the flares were inside the orbit we carved in the air over the jungle. None of the flashes and flares came from the hillside.

"Holeey shit. Nav, NOS. There's flares all over the damn place. Which one's ours?" I glanced at Major McCall beside me. In the flickering yellow light of the flares, his face wore a devilish grin, teeth bright below his bushy mustache. He slapped me on the back gleefully. He's gone crazy, I thought. Maybe I should tell someone up front in the cockpit.

"Bald Head, Bald Head. Stinger 31. We see many flare, many flare. Which flare your flare?" Rich was back on the radio, his pidgin transmissions out-Bald Heading Bald Head.

Beside me, Cash McCall seemed to be choking with laughter. His eyes streamed tears and he was slapping himself in the chest with his gloved hand. He's having a fit, I thought. Good Lord, why me? Why now? From somewhere far below, filled with pride and triumph, Bald Head's voice cut through my confusion. "Aah, Stinger. This Bald Head. Me no shoot flare yet."

Major McCall tried to say something, failed, then reeled aside and collapsed full- length to the cargo compartment floor where he continued to flop and hoot with laughter. Complete combat fatigue, I thought. I knew he had been in gunships a long time and was scheduled to return to the states soon, but I began to feel that he had really gone round the bend, probably never to return.

Bald Head had hardly paused for breath. "Okay Stinger, I shoot flare now."

I centered the NOS on the bare patch on the hillside and sure enough, I caught the bright spurt of flame from a mortar. Above the scarred hillside, the flare popped, sputtered and grew in brightness beneath its parachute.

"That my flare, Stinger. You see my poosition?"

"Nav, NOS, I'm on the position where the flare came up. I caught the mortar flash."

"Roger, NOS."

"Bald Head, Stinger 31. We see your poosition. We see you even when flare goes out. Where you want us to shoot first?"

Finally! I thought. Although it had really not taken long to find the FAG's position, it seemed as if we had wasted half the night. I was ready to go to work. I turned and looked at Major McCall, who had finally struggled back to the NOS door and was looking out. I stared at his face, where the mustache twitched each time he conquered the urge for further silliness.

"Once again the wily Bald Head outfoxes the enemy," he said. "And half his friends. He's a smart son of a bitch. Now we know for sure the bad guys are monitoring our radios. Bald Head probably got a pretty good fix on where those other flares came up from. Now you better figure out which way is north before we start getting targets."

The major was right. I had to orient myself to the terrain below, because Bald Head would probably put us on his targets based on the direction and distance from his location. The problem was that I had no idea of our heading, which changed all the time as we orbited over the target area. The designers of our airplane had not had the foresight to put even so much as a

17

small magnetic compass down at the NOS position. It was a shortfall that would always cause delays as ground troops gave us references to enemy and friendly sites based on compass headings.

As we came around parallel to a small stream that would be a good ground reference, I asked Rich for our heading. I then used the heading to make a mental map of the terrain below, aligned with the cardinal points of the compass.

When Bald Head's flare burned out, I would still be able to see the stream through the NOS, and use that as my reference for north and south, east and west.

"Stinger, Bald Head. You shoot bad guy poosition where I tell you. You see place where machinegun shoot at my poosition? It maybe four hundred meters north from me, where small water joins large water." As Bald Head spoke, his flare finally hit the ground and burned out among the trees. Darkness returned to the jungle.

"Bald Head, Stinger. Stand by, we check."

"Nav, NOS has both the friendly position and what I think he means about water. A big stream and a little one join up pretty near where those green tracers were coming from earlier."

"Okay, NOS. Hold the spot where the streams join and the FLIR will hold on Bald Head's position. Is that machinegun still shooting?"

"Negative, Nav. He quit shooting when the real Bald Head put his flare up."

In the cockpit, Bob Profitt, the other sensor operator, had locked his forward looking infra-red television sight on Bald Head's hillside bunker area. This instrument detected and displayed differences in the temperature of objects in its field of view. The effect for the operator was much like viewing a black and white television screen. The video was presented in varying shades of gray.

The version of this system we carried aboard our aircraft was fairly primitive, and the FLIR was better at finding trucks and other large objects than it was at detecting people. But once an area was pinpointed, as we had with Bald Head's location, the FLIR could easily lock on and hold it. Unlike the NOS, it did not require any ambient light to enable it to detect targets or to see the terrain below.

The table Nav and the FLIR sat side by side where both could see the FLIR scope and the fire control computer. Using the slads (sensor location and depression) indicator, that showed where my NOS was pointing at any time, Bob was able to move and position the FLIR screen crosshairs to the point I tracked on Bald Head's hillside. The FLIR would back me up to make sure we didn't fire on the friendly position.

"Bald Head, Stinger. We ready to shoot now. We pretty sure we see bad guy position. Do you want to shoot tracer at Bad Guy and mark his position for sure?"

"Chi, Stinger. Bald Head shoot."

Immediately, red tracers licked out from Bald Head's hillside and vanished into the jungle at the stream junction we had marked as his target. In return, bursts of green tracers showered back toward Bald Head. Ricochets spun in all directions from the hillside. The bad guys had not moved when they had the chance. Bad luck for them.

"NOS, you got that position?"

"That's affirm, Nav."

"Pilot, Nav. We're all set up. Friendly and enemy positions identified. You've got ten mils coincidence on the sight. NOS is the sensor. We'll try a marking burst first. Master Arm is coming on. You have consent." "Roger, Nav. Understand ten mils coincidence. Gunners, give me number one mini. I'm into the sight. Comin' to ya, NOS."

My left arm extended down the length of the long barrel of the NOS and held it steady in the aircraft slipstream. My right index finger curled around and depressed the trigger to indicate to the fire control computer that I was on target. In the green light of the eyepiece, the pinpoint source of machinegun fire flashed a brighter green under the crosshairs, a yellow flare as the bullets hosed toward the hillside.

I twitched as the gun beside me roared into life. A cascade of fire arced down toward the jungle. Our tracers formed an unbroken rope of red that stretched away below us, tying us to the ground with bullets. Through the NOS eyepiece, I was blinded by the amplified light and released the trigger before I could let the sight wander off target. The pilot called "Out of the sight," and I relaxed for a second.

The gatling gun fired six thousand rounds per minute. Our three second burst rained three hundred bullets into the jungle position. Bald Head was clearly impressed. His happy shouts filled the airwaves.

Some brave soul down there in the enemy position was not so impressed, however. From the same spot in the edge of the jungle, a wavering burst of fire lifted into the air, but not at all near us in our orbit. A surprised and shaken gunner was probably firing at the sound of our engines.

"Nav, Pilot. That son of a bitch is shooting at us again. Are we far enough away from Bald Head to use the twenties?"

"Pilot, Nav. Shouldn't be a problem. We're shooting quite a ways away and we've got a good lock on everybody's location."

"Crew, Pilot, take the mini off and put on number one twenty. I'm into the sight. Comin' to ya, NOS." "Master arm switch corning on. You have consent," Rich said.

I held my breath and kept the trigger depressed for what seemed an age before the pilot finally squeezed his trigger and completed the firing circuit. The Vulcan cannon's roar was a long harsh bellow, twice as loud as the minigun, but the only light it produced was the continuous white hot flame of the muzzle blast. No tracers were loaded in the twenties so this time I was not blinded by our own gunfire. A hundred explosive cannon shells raced earthward in the dark.

In the edge of the jungle, at the junction of two streams, a string of bright flashes winked and died. A tight cluster of explosions covered the source of the green tracers. A tiny flame spurted up brightly and as quickly burned down. This time, there was no return fire.

"Nice pattern," said the FLIR.

***

The clouds were moving in below us and Bald Head's position was becoming hard to see. After dealing with the machine gun, he had directed us from spot to spot to put down more fire. We had received some ground fire and silenced it all. Bald Head referenced all targets in distance and direction from his bunker. Some were as far as two kilometers away. But now, if we were to continue to work with him, we had to maintain visual contact with something on the ground.

"Bald Head, Stinger 31. We want to put ground flare on next target. The clouds make it hard to see your position so we mark bad guy position. Okay?"

"Okay, Stinger. Bald Head copy. You put mark on target 900 meters west my position. Bearing to them is 280 degrees. Bad guys in cave. You put mark by them."

In our left rear cargo compartment door, we carried a flare launcher loaded with twenty-four flares. Six of these were called 'Logs' and, unlike the regular flares, fell directly to earth when launched, rather than floating down under parachute canopies. We used the logs as long lasting visual and infra-red references on the ground. They were handy except when working in deep jungle, where the logs vanished through the tree canopy, never to be seen again.

"NOS, Nav. We're going to rollout and cut across the orbit, directly over Bald Head on a heading of 280. You call the mark for putting the log out. Winds are out of the west at 12 knots. If Bald Head can see the mark on the ground, he can correct our fire from there."

I searched my memory for the handy-dandy formula for dropping the flares and logs. It was a timing problem that depended on our airspeed and the wind direction. I wanted the ground mark to fall 900 meters beyond the spot where Bald Head was bunkered down. We would cross directly over him, directly into the wind, but the log had no parachute to cause a lot of drift. I settled on a release time and made sure I could see my watch's second hand.

"Pilot, Nav. Rollout now, heading 280. NOS, standing by for your call."

"Bald Head, Stinger 31." Rich had switched to the radio to tell the FAG what we were doing. "We fly over you now to drop ground mark, then we shoot."

"Roger, Stinger. This Bald Head."

I was satisfied that I could put the log where it was supposed to go, but the low clouds were causing me real problems, partially hiding the FAG's bunker area. As we got closer to his position, the entire area was obscured by one particularly thick cloud. I decided to estimate when we passed over Bald Head and start my countdown from there. An instant later, I began the mental count and called to our enlisted Illuminator Operator who controlled the flare launcher.

"I.O., NOS, stand by to launch mark. Ready, ready, Launch log."

With a whoosh of compressed air, the log sailed out of the flare launcher. It would not ignite until it was on the ground. The pilot dropped our left wing and we resumed an orbit about where the log should have come down. Through the NOS, I could see the first fiery sputters as the mark ignited.

"Bald Head, Stinger 31. Do you see mark yet?" Bald Head seemed very tentative when he responded. "Aah, Stinger, you shoot mark yet?"

Rich, understanding the FAG to ask if we had already launched the mark, answered, "Chi, Bald Head, we shoot mark. "

There was a very short pause, then a wildly excited Bald Head was back on the radio shouting, "Stinger, don't shoot, don't shoot! You mark my poosition Stinger, you read Bald Head?"

Beside me, Major McCall had once again lapsed into hysterics, but Rich came back on the radio to reassure the FAG.

"Bald Head, Stinger 31. Not to worry. We no shoot your position, but we still use mark to help us find bad guys. No sweat. We move 900 meters west from place we mark.1t

Our fire control computer was capable of computing an offset from a known location so that we could lock on the location with a sensor and fire accurately up to 1000 meters from there. Rich set the up computer and the FLIR locked on the burning log near Bald Head's bunker. After confirming that the correct target was selected, we fired a long cannon burst at the cave site.

As we started a second burst from the other side of the orbit, the copilot excitedly keyed the mike. "We got a fire light! Fire light in the right recip engine!

"That's the right jet, copilot," the flight engineer broke in acidly.

"It's really an overheat light, crew, not a fire light," said the pilot. "Nothing to sweat, but I've had all the fun I can stand for one night, anyway.

"Gunners, give me all guns on line. Nav, tell Bald Head we have a slight problem and we're going home, but we will shoot as we climb up.

"NOS, hold the target as long as you can. Make sure we stay away from Bald Head. I'm in the sight, comin' to ya." I aimed the NOS at our last target and held the trigger as the pilot did the same. All six guns combined in a deafening roar. Four streams of red tracers fell like separate waterfalls toward the jungle cave. A continuous barrage of bright flashes on the ground marked the cannon shells' impact. The whole airplane seemed to sway and yaw sideways in recoil to the volume of lead pouring down. As we climbed through a thin cloud layer, the gunfire's reflection turned the sky around us a hellish flickering red.

As the cloud blotted out the ground, I released the trigger and the pilot pushed the throttles up to begin the long drag home. Rich completed the "after firing check list" and safed the Master Arm switch, before he returned to say goodbye to Bald Head, who was shouting on the radio.

"Stinger, Stinger. You do good work! Good shooting, good shooting! I think you kill [a pause] twenty bad guy! You come back, work with Bald Head again."

"Chi, Bald Head. We like to work with you very much.

We come back, shoot many bad guy. We go home now, but we see you again. Maybe after daylight, you go out, checky-check and see how we do tonight. Let us know."

The response on Bald Head's radio frequency surprised us all. An American voice, complete with Midwestern accent, came back. "Sure, Stinger. We'll checky-check tomorrow. Nighty-night now. You'all come back and see us again."

I shook my head. Major McCall was right. This was a different kind of experience. I wondered if I'd ever really know who Bald Head was or what he was doing out there. There were certainly things going on I didn't understand. I supposed I'd blown my check ride by dropping the log on the friendlies instead of the enemy. But, what could they do to me; send me to Southeast Asia? I was already here. And I'd volunteered.

"Well, Larry. Congratulations. What do you think about close air support?" Major McCall had recovered his composure and once again looked out toward the darkened jungle.

"I think you were right about the radios, sir. But, overall, we seemed to be shooting a long way from the FAG for it to be close air support. And uh, congratulations for what, sir?"

25

"Why, you passed your check ride. Flying colors. Providing you don't break a leg getting out of the airplane back home. And you're right about our shooting not being very close. After we took out the machine gun, Bald Head probably just put us where he thought the bad guys might be forming up or hiding. You'll find that we often get called just to give somebody on the ground some confidence that help is around. Sort of an airborne security blanket. But you never know, if we hadn't been there, there could have been a major attack."

On the way back to Thailand, I sat in the open NOS door as we tried to skirt a line of thunderstorms between us and home. The plane tossed in the rough air and cold rain blew into the open doors and hatches in the cargo compartment. Sitting at my position, soaked and cold, I thought about Bald Head and his troops out in the wet dark, with no support except what he could drum up from our Air Force. And I thought a little about the white explosions clustering around the enemy gun emplacement. But that memory, I decided to put aside for a later time.

All that was left for this mission was to get safely back to that wet runway in Thailand, go through intelligence debrief, sign the grade sheet that said I was now qualified to do my flying job, go to the Officers' Club for eggs, bacon and tequila, and then hit the rack in my air conditioned hootch till noon.

THE ROAD TO NAKHON PHANOM

Now that I was checked out in the aircraft, my life in Thailand fell into a routine that quickly made every day seem like any other. I lost track of the days of the week. The weekend, so important in the States, meant nothing here. The only two times that seemed important were the takeoff time on the next night's flying schedule and what time the flag would be hoisted above the little post office to signify that the mail was in and up.

The high points of the day were mail and the daily trip to the Base Exchange to see what new stereo equipment was available. If we were not on the flying schedule, we might see a movie outside the officers' club. The standard old timer comment heard after any of these movies was "Oh, well. Another two hours out of the tour."

Although I was now flying almost every other night, I was still considered an FNG. This was an abbreviated and acceptable term for Fuckin' New Guy. In polite company FNGs were called "Newbies". Either term meant that I had not yet been around long enough to gain experience in the theater. Being a lieutenant as well as an FNG meant that I would bear watching. My closest friends were those other FNGs who had arrived in-country with me. Even the newly arrived lieutenant colonels were FNGs and we all stuck pretty much together.

I envied the easy camaraderie shared by the troops who had been in-country for a longer period. Later on, I would realize that much of that camaraderie was superficial. It was hard to build esprit when significant portions of the unit regularly departed for the States while less experienced troops remained behind.

Even though it was hard to get to know the people, we rapidly became accustomed to the mission and the equipment. For

27

instance, I no longer considered the aircraft we flew to be the ugliest thing in the air. I had undergone a remarkable change in attitude.

I had volunteered for gunships and, sight unseen, had chosen the AC-119K. This was a cargo and troop carrier aircraft that had known fame in the Korean War as the "Flying Boxcar." Our design engineers had added guns, sensors, extra radios and other frills to the point that the plane could hardly be coaxed off the ground. Of course, no one bothered to tell me that while I was volunteering.

I saw the airplane for the first time on my arrival for training at Hurlburt Field in Fort Walton Beach, Florida. I immediately realized this was not a glamorous airplane. It most closely resembled a black and green Hostess Twinkie with wings. Hatches and doors were open all over the thing and it had an odd assortment of four engines; one big reciprocating (recip) propeller engine on each wing and, outside of each of these, a smaller jet engine. Every time the recips started up, huge clouds of white smoke enveloped the entire airplane, sending startled, coughing onlookers scrambling for air.

The most unusual aspect of the aircraft was that the twinkie-like fuselage was not attached to the tail section. Instead, a long metal cylinder, called a boom, extended rearward from the wing behind each recip engine, parallel to the fuselage. Well behind the fuselage, each boom was topped with a tall vertical stabilizer and rudder. The booms each joined one end of the horizontal tail plane beneath these rudders.

The overall visual effect of the booms and tail assembly, when viewed from directly below, was that of a huge set of football goalposts. Later, I learned that our fliers actually called anti-aircraft rounds which came between the fuselage and tail assembly Field Goals.

Ten men made up the standard crew for this monster. A pilot and copilot sat up front, along with a flight engineer, a table navigator, and the FLIR operator, who was also a navigator. These two navigators sat behind what was humorously known as the "bulletproof curtain," a black felt curtain that prevented the light from the navigator's lamp and the FLIR television screen being seen outside the cockpit.

In the cargo compartment, were the NOS, who was a navigator, three enlisted men called gunners, who maintained and loaded the guns, and the Illuminator Operator, who operated the flare launcher and the one million candlepower spotlight.

In combat areas, the gunners and Illuminator Operator also had the unenviable task of hanging partially out of the two rear paratroop doors, attached to the airplane by nylon safety harnesses, and peering through the cold slipstream to scan for anti- aircraft fire. When flak guns fired on the airplane, the scanners would call the pilot with directions to break away from any accurate fire.

Each break call they made was a judgment call based on experience. The scanner had to be able to evaluate the path of the airplane in its orbit as well as the curving trajectory of the enemy shells. A good, experienced scanner was worth his weight in gold and was, literally, a life saver for his crew. The rest of us learned to estimate how close the flak would be by listening to the pitch of the scanner's voice; the closer the anti- aircraft fire, the higher the pitch.

Our training in Florida progressed rapidly. In three months, we became proficient in the basics of gunship equipment and attack techniques, learned to respect the customs and people of Vietnam and Thailand, and discovered all the good bars in the Florida panhandle. The local populace was good enough to put up with the noise of nighttime cannon fire and the occasional part that fell off our antique airplanes.

They also put up with many of our pranks and experiments with the gunships' equipment. My favorite nighttime victim was the occasional car we discovered hidden in romantic parking spots. In complete darkness, we would enter an orbit around the unwary parkers, align the huge spotlight, then turn it on to bathe the car in a circle of brightness. When the surprised people in the car started up and drove away, we would douse the light and follow. Each time they parked, we repeated the process. We must have been the source of dozens of reports of spacecraft and unidentified lights in the sky.

All too soon our training was over. We graduated and received our orders for Phan Rang Air Base in South Vietnam. We would not travel alone.

***

The way to Vietnam in the early seventies, for most of us, resembled a steadily swelling watercourse. The human tide began as driblets from all areas of the country. It flowed more powerfully from the metropolitan population centers and trickled from the rural areas. The streams joined on the way to the West Coast embarkation points, mixing at airports and bus terminals, growing in volume, accelerating and becoming more forceful in purpose as it neared those single spots where it would leap from our west coast across the Pacific.

Traveling to and returning from Vietnam was like completing a milestone in a continuing education. Each soldier and airman hoped to graduate in a year and, in his turn, be on the plane home with all body parts intact. Because the fighting in Vietnam had gone on so long, this bit of further education, while risky, seemed as inevitable as high school after junior high.

Before early 1972, Air Force flight crewmembers did not seem to depart for Vietnam in combat ready units. The process was rather more piecemeal. Because of our military's policy of each person spending a one-year tour in Southeast Asia, our rotation dates back to the States were known and replacements could be scheduled. When individual replacements went to Southeast Asia, they filled a vacant position made available when someone else rotated home or finished his tour in a more tragic manner. The Air Force went one step beyond when replacing gunship crews. Instead of sending individual replacements, small groups of crewmembers were trained and dispatched overseas as a class.

Our aircrew members had trained together as a class in our gunship weapons system, and together we were shipped as replacements to a particular unit to replace another class which was rotating out of Southeast Asia. We were to assemble at Travis Air Force Base in California for departure. After our gunship training in Florida, we split up for final leave. Then each of us began the journey to Southeast Asia as a single molecule, joined other uniformed molecules along the way, and finally reached Travis to reassemble as a class again. We replacements, either taken individually or as a class, were on our way to a one year combat tour.

***

To us, the departure seemed a very casual military send-off; there were no encouraging speeches or music. We were dispatched by a group of disinterested paper pushers who had already seen too many men and women get on the big planes and head west.

***

Some of my classmates had their wives with them until boarding time. The couples sat quietly in the big terminal area, talking softly, calmly waiting for the time to say goodbye and board the plane. I don't know who was more fortunate, those of us who had already said goodbye, or those whose last sight of their wives was across the turnstiles and wooden barriers separating those who left from those who were left behind.

I said goodbye to my wife at the Dallas-Fort Worth airport. In a sad farewell, Debbie and I had left my parents standing on the front porch of the old farmhouse by the Red River and headed south to a friend's house in Dallas. Debbie's parents met us there and drove us to the airport. They kindly remained in the terminal lobby as Debbie and I headed to the boarding gate. We had little time for conversation before the boarding announcement came, but by then, there was not much left to say. Debbie stood stiff and straight, small chin up, but, one after another, slow teardrops fell like silver rain from behind her dark glasses. I knew I would remember each shining tear as long as I lived.

My family had always had a good luck tradition of never watching a traveler out of sight, so I had asked her to leave before I boarded the plane. With a final solemn kiss, Debbie turned and made her way back along the concourse to the lobby where her parents waited. My eyes followed her until her straight back and black hair were lost among the taller passengers. She never turned to look back. With a sigh, I turned and entered the gate alone and walked down the boarding ramp. My footsteps were unnaturally loud on the plastic floor tiles. I felt lonely but oddly excited, torn between isolation and anticipation. I was making a sacrifice. I was on my way to war, alone. I felt like a hero.

Aboard the jet, I found my seat assignment in the center of a row and next to a young black woman who fidgeted at the window. When she noticed the shiny new navigator wings on my dress uniform, she apologized for her nervousness, and explained that this was her first time to fly. I settled into my seat like an old-timer, stretched easily and told her not to worry, because I'd explain everything to her as we went along. I really felt like a hero.

***

When I reached California, I joined up with Captain Walt King, one of my gunship training classmates. We had been on the same student crew at Hurlburt and were good friends. Walt had been in the Air Force for seven years as a navigator flying Military Airlift Command's heavy transport aircraft. I was sure he knew his way around the Air Force and felt that his experience in MAC would make our long trip overseas easier.

Walt was not an easy person to get to know right away. He was constantly alert to anything that appeared to be a good deal. Many other captains were immediately convinced that he was a first- rate jerk when he introduced himself, "Hi. I'm Walt King. What's your date of rank? I wonder if I outrank you." It was a not always the best way to get off to a good first impression because people did not know if he were joking or not. Walt was a studious, serious, Air Force Academy graduate whose glasses gave him a distinctly bookish appearance. He was a very professional and efficient officer who was a good friend for anyone who took the time to get used to his warped sense of humor.

At Travis Air Force Base, I was reintroduced to Fran, Walt's wife, and his children, who had accompanied him to Florida for training. Before he was drafted for gunships, he had been assigned to Travis and his family would remain in their home in nearby Vacaville while he completed his tour in Vietnam.

Walt and I planned to sit together on the contract airliner that would carry us to the Philippines and jungle survival enroute to our new assignment in Vietnam. I was waiting for him to say goodbye to Fran when the last call for boarding came. Walt had assured me that there was no need for hurry, because the officers would board the plane first, in order of rank, and that there was no need to hustle into line.

When Walt's goodbyes were finally over and we hoisted our carry-on bags, we were the very last in line. To Walt's astonishment, that old axiom, RHIP, Rank Hath Its Privileges, was not in effect on this trip. There were no choice seats left to us, officers or not.

We struggled all the way to the back of the airplane and slipped into the last two seats against the rear bulkhead. Every seat aboard the airliner was now filled. I could see why the old timers called them "cattle cars." In front of us, an ocean of military haircuts extended toward the front of the plane. Most of the men were reclining comfortably, resting prior to takeoff.

When I pushed my seat recline button, the seat seemed stuck in the upright position. I punched the button harder and lunged backward. The only thing to recline was my neck. My head, at the end of the whiplash motion, struck the bulkhead with a thump like a dropped melon hitting the sidewalk. One of the stewardesses working in the galley behind me peered around the corner. I smiled up innocently, eyes crossed. She frowned at me and disappeared around the corner again. A moment later, smiling now, she reappeared and stuffed a pillow between the back of my head and the bulkhead.

"Honey," she said, "these two seats don't recline." That stewardess certainly knew her airplane seats. They didn't recline all the way to the Alaskan air base where we stopped for refueling. Then they didn't recline all the way across the Pacific to Clark Air Base where we were herded off to attend the one week jungle survival course, known throughout the Air Force as Snake School. Walt and I sat bolt upright all the way and listened unwillingly to a young black soldier who, reclining comfortably in the seat in front of Walt, sang rock songs all the way across the pond. Every time I caught Walt's eye, I muttered those magic letters, "RHIP."

***

Snake School was far different from the other survival schools the Air Force had used to enrich our lives. It was much friendlier. The basic survival course had been taught in wintertime Washington State. There we had been thrown into a simulated Prisoner of War camp to teach us resistance techniques, then led on a four day escape and evasion exercise in the snow. Neither the school environment, nor the weather, was warm.

Water survival was easier. The Florida weather at MacDill Air Force Base was suitable for a watery adventure, but the sand fleas, mosquitoes, and many hours in salt encrusted flight suits diminished the pleasure. We did, however, learn much about inflating life rafts and being dragged behind speeding motorboats by parachute lines.

Jungle survival, by contrast, was pretty much a gentleman's class. Instructors were friendly, quarters were satisfactory and the students displayed a tangible willingness to learn. This attitude may have been enhanced by our impending combat exposure, but the Shoot Down Board probably had much more to do with it.

This big display board was the first thing we noticed when we entered the survival school building. It stretched across two walls and included the names of all the Air Force crewmen shot down or otherwise forced to abandon their aircraft in Southeast Asia. It was a mighty impressive list. The instructors pointed out that there were still two walls left for more names.

35

Snake School consisted of three days of classroom academics and two days and a night in the Philippine jungle. The academics passed quickly and then we were divided into small groups for our tour of the jungle. Each group would be shepherded by an enlisted American instructor and a Filipino Negrito. The real teacher was the Negrito. We would meet him later in the jungle.

The trek into the jungle began in the backs of camouflaged trucks which creaked and groaned into the hills, raising clouds of dust and diesel fumes. As we roared through villages, small children ran after the trucks, laughing. Those of us with hard candy or gum pitched goodies to the kids. After a couple of hours, the trucks halted in a clearing, where heavy HH-3 helicopters waited. Each student group boarded a chopper and was carried away to a different landing zone. After a short flight, my group was deposited on a razor-backed ridge between two narrow valleys. As we clambered out of the helicopter, we were greeted by a Negrito, taller than average, who introduced himself to us as Mike.

Even with broken English, Mike was one of the most expressive persons I ever met. He showed us plants to avoid, like the fire tree which imparts painful burns to anyone unwary enough to brush against it.

We learned that his father had fought the Japanese in the jungles. Once, pantomiming mixing tree sap in water, he explained, "My father kill many Japanese this way. You need make poison, this plant good."

Mike led us to edible plants as well. He selected a vine looping between two close growing trees, and using his long machete, slashed a section free. When he tilted the section of vine, satisfying water flowed from the fresh cut.

After our first day of training, we camped for the night. Mike used a section of large bamboo for a cooking pot and brewed a delicious stew made of plants he had gathered during the day and a small canned ham one of us smuggled along in our pack. We shared the friendly atmosphere of a Boy Scout cookout.

Everyone was quite festive around the fire, but when we dispersed to our hammocks and mosquito nets, some of the group decided to stay awake and feed the fire. They were rather put out by the true stories of the large rats that haunted the jungle. These nocturnal creatures were attracted by the scent of food. One member of an earlier class had been bitten on the lip by a rat who liked the smell of peanut butter.

My bed down area was farther downhill and separated from the camping area by a screen of trees. I used my penlight to find my way down the hill and into the grove where I had slung my hammock. Above me on the hill, the men who elected to remain awake amused themselves by shooting pen gun flares at a group of students on the next ridge across the valley. I hardly noticed the return fire falling around my jungle bedroom. I was fast asleep as soon as I climbed in and adjusted the mosquito net.

When my rowdy classmates and their pen gun flares couldn't disturb my rest, nature stepped in to make sure I enjoyed the jungle night to the fullest. From the dark above, came a terrible cry and one of the trees supporting my hammock shivered from the impact of a large body.

My eyes jerked open to the dark and I lay frozen in my hammock. Leaves and twigs rained down on my mosquito net. "Whooaaahh," the deafening whoop rang out right above my head. Something was spiraling down through the tree limbs above me. Every time it struck a limb, it emitted a shrieking honk and more debris fell on my bed.

Then, I could hear the wings. Leathery sounding wings were beating the air, Ka-flap, the wing beats seeming to be two or three seconds apart. That must mean it had a huge wingspan. Good God, I thought, a flying dinosaur lives in the jungle and it's after me. I cowered in the hammock as the thing finally broke free of the tree limbs and pulled out of its fall just above my hammock. With a final Ka-flap that brushed the mosquito netting, it sailed off down the hill, whooping and blundering into other trees in the dark.

In a book about World War II in the Philippines, I had read of just such a bird, but I had never even considered being unlucky enough to encounter one. But luck was really with me this night, because twice more, the bird, or one just like it, retraced its path, hammering into trees and showering the jungle floor with squawks and refuse.

The training for the next morning centered on using the jungle to evade capture. Mike demonstrated. We all turned our backs, and in a moment, Mike found a hiding place in our clearing. Our American instructor told us when to begin to search for him. Although Mike had hidden himself within yards of the rest of us, we did not find him. Finally, with a big grin, he crawled out of a small patch of brush not much bigger than his body. Somehow he had managed to look like just another part of the jungle floor.

The final part of our jungle training was the live escape and evade exercise. We students would have approximately half an hour to hide in the valley. Then the searchers would be turned loose to find us. The survival school contracted with several Negrito villages in the area to provide men to beat the jungle to find the evaders. Each student was issued two chits, each good for one bag of rice. When a student was discovered by a Negrito tribesman, he surrendered a chit to the Negrito who could then cash it in for the rice.

Our instructors led us down the steep ridge to the valley floor where all the student groups were assembled. We could see the dark faces and white teeth of dozens of Negritos at the far end of the valley, waiting the chance to collect rice from the Yankees. Opposite the tribesmen, the valley was thick with tall grass and brush. Along the base of the ridge behind us, a stream made pleasant watery sounds. I was planning which direction I would take, when we got the word to go. Like a flash, I was off through the tall grass, running like crazy. All around me, classmates were fanning out in every direction.

True to my plan, I cut through the tall grass, leaving a path of broken and crushed vegetation. When I guessed I had gone far enough, I doubled back and carefully turned aside from the trail of flattened foliage. I crawled carefully, trying to leave no marks, until I reached the base of some small bushes where I rolled over on my back. Behind me, I could see no indications that I had come this way. I felt secure, so I leaned back to rest. Suddenly, wild screams split the air from the other end of the valley. That half hour had gone by like a flash and the hungry Negritos were on the loose. Simultaneously with the screams, some small buggy creature fell from an overhanging limb directly into my right eye. But, I was not going to let a little thing like pain stop me. I stayed in my hide, rubbing my eye.

All around me, the sounds of the searchers grew louder. The Negritos called to each other and, in an effort to scare us from our hiding places, made long whooping noises. It seemed that most of the pack was passing by my hiding place. The whoops were past and going away.

Behind me, the grass stirred faintly. I whirled around to see a smiling native parting the brush with his long machete. I stood up, handed over a rice chit and started back to the stream to find the instructor and get the bug out of my eye. The Negrito headed away at a trot, after more chow.

After the instructor got the small spider out of my eye, I looked for another hiding place. Negritos rambled all over the valley and would probably see me if I went back out to the grass to hide. Instead, I wandered behind a screen of trees and found one I could climb. It was a small tree, but up about twelve feet, there was a broad limb I could stand on, and another that made a good rest for my elbows.

Before long a Negrito showed up. He paused beneath my tree and sniffed. I looked down between my feet at him as he turned his head from side to side, listening carefully. While I held my breath above, he called out a long low "Wheeeeyouuu." His bewilderment was easy to read; this man knew there was someone hiding out nearby, but the thought of looking up in the tree never crossed his mind. With a shrug and a cautious look around he started out at a trot.

Seconds later a pair of searchers stopped beneath my tree and went through the same routine. I had momentary thoughts of hopping down out of the tree to surprise them, but the sight of their long machetes changed my mind. Then, I had to strangle the strong urge to call down to them, "Wheeeeyouuu." Only the pride of outfoxing them stopped me. They left at last, and I climbed down, found the skinniest Negrito around and handed him my second rice chit. Then I joined the instructors and those students who had been discovered and were now out of rice chits. In an hour we were aboard the helicopters and on the way back to base.

At two in the morning, we were seated in canvas seats aboard an Air Force transport on our way to Vietnam. Our first stop in Southeast Asia was Da Nang Air Base in South Vietnam. There, we learned our assignment base had been changed to Nakhon Phanom Royal Thai Air Base, in northeastern Thailand. None of us complained. Nakhon Phanom was called NKP by the Americans who lived there. Others called it the Country Club.

There were no jet fighters at NKP. The 56th Special Operations Wing ran NKP and every aircraft stationed there was either a helicopter or else had at least one propeller. The Al-E Skyraider aircraft were propeller driven attack planes that were used for supporting the rescue of downed aircrew members. The HH-53 Jolly Green Giant rescue helicopters flew out of NKP as well. The OV-10 Bronco Forward Air Control (FAC) aircraft were small twin turboprop planes used to direct air support for ground units. And NKP was the home of the 18th Special Operations Squadron, who owned our AC-119K Stingers.

NKP was in a very rural area near the muddy Mekong River. Across the Mekong, the jungles of Laos hid the enemy we would seek at night. The Thai jungles came right to the edge of our own runways and, after dark, we all would learn to keep a wary eye out for cobras or other snakes. We accepted Nakhon Phanom with open arms. It was a swell place compared to anywhere in Vietnam.

At NKP there were usually thirteen full gunship crews on hand. Each crew flew combat missions into Laos several times a week. We FNGs were not initially assigned to a regular crew. We filled in positions on other established crews when someone was sick or taking time off for some other reason.

In northern Laos, we usually flew into an area we called Barrel Roll. This included an area of flat uplands known as the Plaine Des Jarres, a name we shortened to PDJ. Supposedly, the inhabitants had at one time buried their dead in large jars which were scattered around the level plains. For us the PDJ provided good truck hunting because of the many trail networks criss-crossing the area.

Barrel Roll was not so heavily defended as the Steel Tiger area to the east and south, because it was further from North Vietnam. There were no SAMs in Barrel Roll, but the anti-aircraft artillery guns went up to 57mm and the 23s and 37s were common. This triple-A was sited in convenient spots along the trail network. The truck drivers all knew where their flak guns were located and when attacked would often drive breakneck over the rough trails until they neared a nest of guns. Then they stopped and abandoned the truck until the air attack was over. I could visualize them hunkered down behind a rock, cheering their gunners on.

Occasionally, we would be sent into the wild area of eastern Laos code named Steel Tiger. The famous siege of the Marine fire base at Khe Sanh had occurred in South Vietnam across the border from the Steel Tiger area. Steel Tiger was heavily defended and another gunship, an AC- 130 Spectre, had been lost there to a SA-2 surface to air missile (SAM) site that had gone undetected. This loss occurred the day I arrived in country. Welcome to the war.

Our sorties were almost all flown after dark. The first aircraft would take off about dusk and the last would land about daylight. Often our aircraft would work so close to the Laotian border that we could see the anti-aircraft fire from the guns defending the Ho Chi Min trail. It could be a spooky sight to watch the 23mm and 37mm tracers spurt into the air and see the bright flashes of the exploding shells. It was especially spooky when we knew that in a few hours we would be above the trail and those same guns would be hurling explosives at us.

The Night of the Field Goals began like that. On the way to the little Thai restaurant on base, Walt and I stopped to watch the first of our evening sorties take off and orbit the base, then head into the deepening dusk to the East. It was not dark enough yet for the black paint on the bottom of the aircraft to hide its silhouette.

"Well, Walt," I said. "I'm flying the third go with Crew 13 tonight. I don't know why in hell they don't just get another crew number and skip that one. They do that with the thirteenth floor on buildings, don't they?"

"Ah, don't be so superstitious," Walt responded. "The pilot on that crew has a good reputation." "He's a professional in the air, all right, but he's a hell-raiser on the ground. Anyway, back to crew numbers, I'd still prefer a number with a better reputation."

After a quick dinner, we paused on the way back to our hootch. On the eastern horizon, we could see the bright flashes of triple-A bursting at altitude and the occasional AAA tracer burning its way into the sky. It looked like a pretty heavy engagement. At this distance and in the darkness, we couldn't see the target airplane. Nor could we tell when Stinger fired. When truck hunting in Laos, we fired only the 20mm Vulcan cannon, which did not use tracers that would give our position away in the firing orbit.

As I pulled on my green, fire resistant flight suit for the mission, I heard the roar and whine of the next Stinger taking off. I stepped outside to watch as it, too, turned and headed to the east. I finished dressing by pulling on green canvas sided jungle boots and headed to the bus stop to catch the small van we called the TUOC Trolley for a ride to the Tactical Unit Operations Center for our intel briefing.

I joined several other members of Crew 13 as we showed our line badges and were cleared past the armed guard into the TUOC. Inside we filed into the briefing room and Capt. Courtney called the roll. Ten crewmembers were all present and accounted for. Then the briefing officers gave us the lowdown.

The weatherman said that tonight he expected our working areas to be clear until well past midnight, with a chance for a line of thunderstorms to build and move in from the east in the early morning hours. Weather back home would be good at our landing time. The moon would set early tonight, so the full darkness would provide good cover. We had no questions.

Then the young female intelligence officer we called Peppermint Patty gave us the big picture on the big news in Southeast Asia. Patty came complete with freckles and red hair and was our favorite thing about intel briefing and debriefing.

She began by telling us how the war was going in the south. We were all familiar with the North Vietnamese effort we were beginning to call the Easter Invasion. Beginning in the early hours of Good Friday, March 30, 1972, the North Vietnamese launched a series of attacks down the length of South Vietnam. More than 100,000 communist soldiers were committed from across the borders of North Vietnam, Laos and Cambodia. Things were grim indeed for the South Vietnamese. There were few American ground units left to help shore up the South Vietnamese Army. The fastest support America could put back into the theater was air power. Fighter units were coming back to Thai bases and the Navy was bringing more carriers to the South China Sea. But right now, the most effective weapon to blunt the invasion was the American planes on hand. A detachment of our squadron aircraft had been operating for some time out of Da Nang. Another would be formed soon to fly from Bien Hoa Air Base, near Saigon.

The current development that affected our missions tonight was the discovery of a large truck park to our east along a side branch of the Ho Chi Minh trail. All sorties tonight were hitting this area.

Patty pointed to the large wall map and indicated several ridges along the trail system. "Triple-A fire is reported heavy from these ridges. Our first sortie saw 23mm and 37mm. There may be 57mm. as well. These AAA sites and lots of machine guns are pretty far up on the ridgeline, so don't count on flying just a little higher to get out of small arms range.

"There are no friendlies in the area. If you are hit and have to bailout, head southwest and get as far as you can out of the trail system. Any questions?"

There were none.

Patty then gave us the Escape and Evasion (E&E) code words and numbers. Should we have to step out of the aircraft over Laos, we would need to be able to authenticate our identity for Search and Rescue forces. At the TUOC, we also maintained identifying materials, but in a hurry, the SAR folks might not have time to check them. I wrote the codes on the palm of my hand in ballpoint ink. If I did not E&E successfully, I could lick or rub them off to protect the codes.

When everyone else had cleared the room, we had a quick crew briefing and then headed for the personal equipment shop to pick up our flight and survival gear. In the PE shop, each crewmember had a bin and a rack for his helmet, parachute and harness, and his survival vest. The helmet was camouflaged green and brown. Because we did not fly high enough to require oxygen, instead of an oxygen mask, we had a boom microphone attached to the side of the helmet.

The survival vest contained a number of pockets which held gadgets designed to get you out of the jungle alive. The most important of these were the two survival radios. Other items were plastic covered maps, mirrors, compass, tracer bullets, whistle, and many other pieces of gear a Boy Scout would have loved to own.

We also carried what we called Pointy-Talkies, which were small pamphlets showing common phrases we might use with corresponding phrases printed in several languages. Of course, the Pointy-Talkie presupposed that we could find someone to show it to who would not first shoot us, and also that the person we found could read. Neither of these suppositions was likely where we were going tonight.

Finally, we had our blood chit. An American flag with a registration number was printed on cloth. Should we find someone to take a message for us, the number on the flag would identify us to American authorities. The writing on the blood chit promised a monetary reward for helping us.

At least we were told this was what it meant, for none of us could translate any of the languages represented on the cloth.

When we were properly attired and equipped, we filled our water bottles, checked our radios, and checked out our .38 caliber revolvers from the armory sergeant. He gave us the gun we were registered for and six bullets. The sergeant also made sure we loaded the gun in the proper manner, which was by pointing it into a big barrel of sand as we fed the bullets into the cylinder. He made sure we understood there would be no excuse if any of us clumsy aircrew oafs accidently shot someone.

Then, finally, we were ready to go to our plane. When we walked out of the PE shop, nobody's mother would recognize him. My normal six foot height was elevated to six-two by boots and helmet and I grossed about ten pounds more than my regular 160. The skull cap I wore beneath the helmet hid my brown hair except a few strands that stuck out over my forehead. At least, I thought, my eyes matched nicely with the rest of my green ensemble. With all my gear, I thought I looked like Steve Canyon and Batman rolled into one.

The crew van unloaded us all at our airplane and we climbed aboard to complete the preflight of our sensors and other equipment. I hung my parachute carefully on the hook by my NOS so that I would be able to find it in the dark. All the crewmembers except the two pilots wore chest pack parachutes with separate harnesses. We could not work freely in the cargo compartment wearing a back pack parachute and an accidentally deployed chute back there in the wind stream would be disastrous. Should the time ever come to use the chest pack chute, we would simply tighten the crotch straps of the harness we wore over our survival vests and clip the parachute on.

When we had gone through the checklists and verified that the fire control computer and sensors were all working as advertised, we met at the back of the airplane. Smokers moved farther away, watching carefully for snakes, to enjoy one last puff before takeoff. At stations time, all ten crewmembers lined the edge of the parking ramp for a last good luck piss and boarded the plane. I never learned the origin of that tradition, but it must have seemed odd to anyone able to watch, that ten serious grown men were all standing, line abreast in the dark, taking a whiz.

At engine start time, we spun the big props. Oily white smoke blanketed the area, the crew chief ran coughing for cover, and we taxied away to the end of the runway. There we started the jets, ran up all engines to maximum power, and with blue flame leaping from the exhaust stacks, roared down the strip.

Once airborne, we circled the base to align our sensors and confirm that the sensors and fire control computer system were cooperating with one another. Our alignment complete, we headed into Laos. When we found an open area that was known to be clear of any friendly Laotians, we took up an orbit around it and completed a "wet boresight" by firing our cannon and tweaking the computer for best accuracy. Finally, we headed east toward the truck park and the triple-A.

The navigator planned our approach to the target area in great detail. The network of trails feeding the truck park ran east and west in this area. We wanted to cut across the trail at a right angle near the park to minimize the tracking time of any AAA guns hiding out on the steep ridgelines along the road. At the same time, if we positioned ourselves correctly, both the NOS and the FLIR could have a good look directly down the trail into the truck park area. This would give us the best possible view of the trail and cut down on the screening effect of the tall trees that masked the trail on either side.

When we crossed the first ridge protecting the trail, the pilot spoke excitedly into the interphone, "Look at the fires, they're everywhere. Our guys have been hitting 'em hard."

A second later I realized that he could only see a portion of the destruction. I was staring through the NOS down a section of trail and every detail was visible. The road was brilliantly illuminated by the hulks of burning trucks parked on each side. The light exposed the full extent of the truck park. Under the tall trees, more vehicles were blazing. The image suddenly vanished as we crossed the next ridgeline, but the smoky smell of burning tires remained with the airplane.

The Triple-A guns which we knew were there did not fire as we cut across above them. They might have been surprised, but more likely they were waiting for us to come back and try to pick off more vehicles.

The Nav came up on the interphone, "Pilot, Nav. Come left, heading 290. We'll run back along the road to the west."

The left wing dipped into the turn. From my NOS door, I could see an orange glow that outlined the ridgeline between us and the blazing truck park.

"Chances are that the word's out by now that we've found this target," the Navigator continued. "For sure, any truck driver getting close has seen the other gunships working out and he ought to be able to see the glow from the fires back there.

"We can do a little road recce back here and I'll bet we find more trucks that are stopping short and trying to find places to hide before they get to the park. If we can't find any, then we can go back and see what the other Stingers left for us."

It sounded like a good plan to me. Besides, those guns back there are already pissed off, I thought.

They were probably just waiting for us to come back, settle into an orbit and become a good target.

"Nav, Pilot. Sounds good to me. What heading do you want? "

"Come left another ten degrees, Pilot. We'll flop over the ridgeline and pick up the trail with the sensors and do a little road recce.

"NOS, you'll be primary sensor. Scan ahead as far as you can. The FLIR will look for hot spots in the trees across the trail from us. When you pick up the trail system, call it and direct us along it, but offset to the north."

"Roger, Nav. NOS copies."

Road Reconnaissance was a familiar truck hunting procedure. It had been the technique we practiced the most in training at Hurlburt. One of the sensor operators directed the aircraft along the road, looking ahead for traffic. At intervals, we would make a single orbit over the trail so the sensors could get a good look up and down the road as we crossed perpendicularly. Then we would roll out on our original heading along the road to check another section of trail. From above, the maneuver would look like a series of horizontal loops across the trail system.

Through the NOS, I saw the ridgeline vanish beneath the aircraft, and there ahead of us the shadowed trail ran like a black scar through the trees. There were no lights visible in the green circle of the NOS eyepiece.

"Nav, NOS. Trail's in sight. No traffic visible.

"Pilot, NOS, come right about ten."

The plane rolled a little to the right and brought our course roughly parallel to the trail. Every few moments, I gave small heading changes to keep us in position. When we came abreast a small clearing, I held the spot in my NOS and we entered our first orbit over the trail. Nothing. After one orbit, we rolled out again and headed west along the jungle road.

"Nav, FLIR. Take a look at this hot spot, could be a truck engine." The FLIR was indicating a point of interest. Instantly, I could sense the crew's attention level growing in anticipation that we might find something to shoot.

On the FLIR's screen, a spot of greater infra-red energy would be displayed as a white dot against the surrounding grey. There was no guarantee that a hot spot meant vehicles, however. It could be a rain-filled bomb crater that was warmer than the roadway, or it could be a large animal.

"NOS, pick a point down there.

"Pilot, Nav, take up orbit, NOS selected. We'll check this out."

I selected a tree taller than others and centered it under the NOS crosshairs. The pilot racked the plane into a steep left turn and we entered orbit.

"NOS, FLIR. Look east down the trail from where you're holding about 500 meters. On the south side of the road, there's a little notch in the tree line and the hot spot is in that little notch. See if you see any light or fire."

Knowing that the pilot would hold steady in his orbit, I swung the NOS down the road to the east and measured off about 500 yards in my aiming reticule. The FLIR, looking at the slads panel and the NOS symbol on the fire control computer, coached me on toward the spot he was watching. I could see a gap in the trees, but nothing else. Anything parked in the gap was hidden by the crowding jungle.

"FLIR, NOS. No joy. There's nothing giving off any light in this area, but I can't see back underneath the trees. If he's in there, he's in the dark."

"Pilot, Nav. We'll try this target out. Elevation is about 3,200 feet. Maintain 5,700 for Charlie altitude. Nearest high terrain is east of us about eight miles, at 6,000 feet. Check altimeters, 29.90."

The pilot and copilot verified their altimeter settings. In the firing orbit, crew coordination was essential. The accuracy of the entire firing operation was a complex juggling of airspeed, bank angle and altitude above the target. The pilot controlled the bank angle of the wings. The copilot controlled the altitude by pulling back and pushing forward on the control yoke. The flight engineer, seated between them on an empty ammo can, controlled the airspeed by advancing or pulling back the four throttles.

Crew coordination to make the guns fire was just as important between the navigator, sensor operators and the gunners in the rear of the airplane. Everyone was responsible for the correct positioning of at least one switch to make the guns fire. The navigator, in his role as fire control officer, would not close the Master Arm switch until he was sure that the entire firing solution looked right. He also set up the fire control computer so that if the pilot's gunsight pipper wandered too far from the dot representing the sensor's aim point, the guns would automatically cease firing. The allowable difference between the two pippers was called the coincidence setting.

Next, the guns would only fire as long as the sensor operator tracking the target kept his trigger depressed. Finally, the gunners had to set their switches correctly to enable the individual cannon and miniguns selected to fire on the target. Essentially, everyone had a trigger. A pilot's call of "No guns" as he pressed the trigger was very frustrating for everyone.

"Okay, Gunners, give me number one twenty.

"FLIR, Pilot. I'm into the sight." A pause, then "Coming to you, FLIR."

Beside me, the cannon fired, its six rotating barrels spinning into a blur. The muzzle flash from the Vulcan was continuous. The bull-roarer voice of the gun ate through my helmet earphones to drown all other sound. The roar seemed to go on for ages. The smell of hot cordite filled the cargo compartment and expended 20mm brass shell casings showered into the big catch tub under the gun.

In the gap along the tree line below, the dark ground flashed and sparkled with the 20mm cannon shells' impact. Still there was no answering spurt of flame or secondary explosion.

"Out of the sight, FLIR." The pilot's voice showed relief from the tension of holding the two gunsight pippers together. "Any hits?"

"Good hits, pilot. Started about ten high and walked right down on the hot spot. Sparkle all over the target, but no reaction."

"NOS, Nav. Can you see any fire or light down there?"

"Negative, no light, Nav." As I spoke, my voice rang hollow in ears still reverberating with the noise of the 20mm gun.

"Okay, pilot, let's try 'er again," the Nav said evenly. "This time, if we don't get any results, we leave." "Roger that, Nav.

"Okay, FLIR, Pilot. I'm into the sight. Comin' to you. "

Once again, the Vulcan roared into life. This time the pilot squeezed off a short burst, then after rolling into a steeper bank, fired again.

"BREAK LEFT! BREAK LEFT! BREAK LEFT!" The scanner's break call came over the intercom almost as a scream.

Our gunfire ceased instantly as the pilots cranked the yoke hard to the left. As the flight engineer shoved the throttles full forward, the engine noise howled up the scale and the old plane seemed to sprint forward. At the NOS door, I watched the left wingtip drop toward vertical and felt the G force increase as the pilot pulled the yoke back into his stomach. I released the NOS and gripped each door side like a gymnast doing the iron cross on swinging rings. Outside the door, the huge propeller seemed to be spinning close enough to fray my flight suit. The increased turn rate made the hazy jungle rush past the door like scenery in a movie at fast forward.

I knew that we were breaking away from triple-A and that it must have come from outside our orbit. I would have been able to see anything come up from inside our turn. Waiting blindly to see how close the triple-A would come was horrible. Each second seemed a dragging hour as we continued the hard turn. We had turned through at least 90 degrees and the nose of the aircraft was now pointed almost south. We were squarely over the trail network and headed toward a ridge that loomed darkly in the haze below.

"ROLL OUT! ROLL OUT!" The scanner's voice was not so shrill this time, merely loud.

"Rolling out, now. We're heading 165. What heading do you want, Nav?" the pilot sounded relaxed on the interphone and the wings were coming smoothly back toward level flight.

I glanced ahead at the ridge that was about to go under our nose. Once past that, we would be out of the trail complex and could plan our next move. Obviously, if we went back to the target in the notch of trees, we would have to be alert for the AAA position that had just chased us off.

Below and ahead of me, halfway up the ridge, a pinpoint of red light popped into existence. It seemed to grow larger and brighter but remained fixed at the same point on the ground. A cluster of red lights, like highway flares, formed around it, growing brighter and larger in the same strange way. It was fascinating. Somewhere in my foggy brain, a synapse fired and a dim light came on.

"BREAK RIGHT! BREAK RIGHT!" My squawk sounded like a panicked chicken, but no one questioned it. The power slammed in and I grabbed the door again, this time to keep from falling backward, as the pilot slammed the airplane into an uncoordinated right turn. Now the right wing was pointed at the ground and I was looking up at the sky.

Outside the NOS door a sudden light show appeared. A formation of red golf balls streaked by, so close they lit up the inside of the cargo compartment. The supersonic crack as the shells went by was like stitches ripping in a taut canvas sail. High above us I saw the flak burst, a series of bright white flashes.

More supersonic cracks. Louder. This time I couldn't see the tracers, but far above us came the series of white flashes.

"Field Goal, three times!" The I.O. was getting his money's worth, tonight. The field goal call meant the shells came up between our fuselage and the twin tail booms. They would have been close to where he hung into the slipstream, watching the guns shoot at us.

"Let me know when I can rollout, Scanner," The pilot called anxiously. If we kept turning we would soon be back over the first gun to fire at us. In the bank we were in, I couldn't even see the ridge where the latest gun was located.

"Pilot, NOS, rollout heading northwest." That seemed the safest direction. To head east again would put us in range of both guns. The wings rolled swiftly back level and the pilot's voice came over the interphone. "Crew, check in. Anybody hurt?"

Each crewmember responded with his position and status. "Well, gentlemen," the pilot said. "I believe we have just experienced a Flak Trap. Maybe that FLIR hot spot was just a fire under an old truck body. They waited for us to commit to the attack and then hosed us.

"Now, Nav, we need a heading and a plan."

"Roger, Pilot. Head 245. We'll continue to recce the trail. We have about half an hour of playtime left. Then we'll head home. In the meantime, I'll call Cricket and pass them the info about the suspected flak trap."

As we headed west, I directed the road recce. Twenty minutes went by, filled with our orbit, move, orbit, progress down the trail. As we completed the fourth circle above the trail, the NOS scope picked up a pair of dim headlights, pointed east along the trail. Apparently, the driver had not seen the earlier fireworks display, or perhaps he thought the guns had driven us out of the area.

"Nav, NOS. Got headlights heading this way. I'm on them now."

"Roger, NOS. Bringing the FLIR over to look, too. Looks like there are three trucks, moving single file, about fifty meters apart. We'll give you first crack, NOS.

"Pilot, Nav. Take NOS guidance and set up an orbit. We've got ten minutes of playtime left."

While the pilot set up the orbit around my target, the navigator gave the target area briefing. In seconds, we were ready to fire. The trucks continued to trundle blindly down the rough road. Behind the lead truck I could faintly make out the shapes of two other vehicles, moving without lights. They were completely oblivious to the black-painted aircraft above them. The sound of the trucks' grinding engines covered the sound of our engine noise.

"Into the sight, NOS." A second later, "Comin' to you."

I was aiming ahead of the moving truck, using Kentucky windage. The only formula I remembered to compute an aim point had nothing to do with shooting. It was the one from Drivers' Education class for computing safe following and stopping distance. I couldn't remember any others. I figured the truck was going about 10 MPH so I moved the crosshairs about one truck length in front of the headlights. At least it was supposed to work in Drivers' Ed.

This time, when our cannon fired, I was ready and didn't flinch. When the firing began, I kept the crosshairs steady rather than moving them along ahead of the truck. The headlights moved slowly from the edge of the green eyepiece toward the center. When the first 20mm rounds struck, the headlights were directly under the crosshairs.

The burst of cannon fire was a long one. The familiar cluster of white flashes blinked like firecrackers all around the headlights. They continued to move for a moment, then veered off the trail and stopped, cutting two bright swathes into the trees. Seconds later, yellow flames sprang up from the edge of the trail and the headlights died.

"Pilot, Nav. Take FLIR guidance. We need to get the third truck in line now and block the one in the middle."

"Roger, Nav. Taking FLIR guidance." The pilot sounded excited on the intercom. "Into the sight. Comin' to you."

Once again, the Vulcan fired, and the bright stars of explosions blossomed on the ground one hundred meters behind the fire in the trees. This time the target truck stopped but would not burn. After two more bursts into the truck, the FLIR moved to the remaining truck, trapped between the first and second targets. This driver probably abandoned his vehicle. It remained stalled in the middle of the trail where our guns blasted it into junk. Soon, it too was enveloped in flame. We had hit the three trucks in exactly ten minutes. It was time to go home.

***

When we got to intel debrief, Peppermint Patty was long gone. We told the intel folks all we saw, marked locations on maps and finished the ton of required paperwork, then headed for chow.

Since we flew at night, our meal schedule was out of step with all the daytime fliers. Fortunately, the Officers' and Enlisted Clubs were open twenty-four hours a day. It was after three a.m. when we arrived. The Thai waitresses didn't seem to mind. They knew us well, for at the times we ate, the rest of the club was usually empty. Tonight, we five officers from the Stinger crew had the place to ourselves. We were in a jolly mood and, after our meal and some small quantity of tequila, the pilot suggested we go serenade the WAF barracks.

The Womens' Air Force, or WAF, officers and enlisted personnel were an important part of the base organization. They were also the only round eye, or non-Asian, women on base. Since most of them were enlisted, and officers were forbidden to fraternize, they were an unattainable but irresistible target for the young officers. The pilot felt that, if we couldn't fraternize with them, at least we could charm them with a couple of old ballads. He dismissed the fact that it was now half past four in the morning. To the rest of us it just sounded like the reasonable thing to do.

The WAF barracks was just across the street from the hootches where most of us lived, so in moments we were on our drunken way, dodging cracks in the sidewalk that looked like snakes, and staggering away from the tall grass where vipers might lurk.

When we arrived at the WAF barracks, we were somewhat at a loss. The building was a long, low, single story contraption, elevated slightly on tall foundation blocks to keep the floors above the monsoon flooding. The front door of each room opened to the slatted wooden porch that ran the length of the building. There were a few yellow lights that illuminated the front doors, but not a single light was on in any of the rooms. There seemed to be no available bodies to hear our serenading.

"Not to worry," whispered our pilot. "We'll just wake some of them up by tapping softly. But, be damned careful that you don't wake up that grouchy old female major. She'll have our asses for messing with the good looking ones."

None of us knew in which room we might find the grouchy major, but picking a door at random, we each tapped softly, then jumped off the porch to form up our Stinger Quintet on the grass.

Our first effort was to be "Where Have All the Flowers Gone," and we started it quietly. In front, the pilot, smiling absently, led the music, blond hair falling over freckled forehead, glazed blue eyes fixed on the barracks doors above us. Door hinges creaked and a couple of tousled heads peeked through the cracks. Our voices grew louder. More heads. Some doors opened all the way and young women in robes and shorts stepped onto the porch. They were beautiful.

We were to the "Where have all the young girls gone" part. More of them came out. Some of them were starting to sing. God bless you, Peter, Paul and Mary. All the male voices faltered as one WAF in short shorts and some kind of skimpy top broke from the pack and tiptoed down the porch to tap on another door. A redhead came out to join the choir. The soft female voices blended wonderfully.

Now, we were to the "Gone to Young Men, Everyone" part.

The singing was much louder. The women were really getting into it. Suddenly, they stopped short. From around the corner had come a bathrobe. In it was a tall woman, spare, with a grey complexion under the yellow bug lights. Old. And very unhappy. We could tell by the way she was grinding her teeth together. We ran like the wind.

Fortunately, my hootch door was unlocked. Inside, Walt, my hootchmate, was snoring softly. The pilot and I slipped inside, locked the door and peeked out through the edge of the blackout curtains. A security police car was stopped in front of the WAF barracks, lights flashing. The sky cops got out and talked to the grouchy old major, who was the only female left on the WAF's front porch. She pointed at our hootch, but the security cop just shook his head. He wasn't about to go pound on the doors of the aircrew quarters. He knew that we fliers needed our rest. The officers got back in their car and left.

Across the way, the major stalked back around the corner. A moment later, from the WAF barracks, a sweet female voice called softly, "Hey, Where Have All the Soldiers Gone?" "We should have started with the 'Old Gray Mare'," the pilot said.

***

The next morning I saw Terry Courtney at the post office. "Larry, I heard this morning that my crew is going to the detachment down at Bien Hoa. Our regular NOS is still sick. You've been assigned to fly with us." I was flattered. "Sure, Terry. Sounds interesting."

MEETING THE EASTER INVASION

Bien Hoa was not a pretty place. Fifteen miles north and east of Saigon, it was a combination of dusty asphalt and jet noise. Since the start of the Easter Invasion, American and South Vietnamese attack aircraft had flown nonstop during the day to bomb and strafe the enemy troops and armor advancing everywhere against the demoralized South Vietnamese ground forces. At night, supply planes brought in more men, more equipment, and more bombs and ammunition.

As we walked from our aircraft parking area to the small building that served as our operations area, a pair of Navy A4- D Skyhawk fighters taxied past, noses bouncing lightly over bumps in the taxiway. The fully extended landing gear struts testified that the airplanes were almost empty of fuel. Black streaks of gun smoke stained the fuselage behind their cannon. They would refuel and rearm and fly a mission on their way back to their aircraft carrier. Air Force F4 Phantom fighters were heading out to the runway, sharks teeth and eyes painted on their long noses. They would line up for take-off behind Vietnamese Skyraiders and American Forward Air Controllers in little 0-2 propeller aircraft who would direct the strikes on enemy positions. The air stank of burning kerosene.

Our ops center was little more than a shack near the flightline. In it were a briefing room with a wall map of South Vietnam and Cambodia, a duty desk with telephones and radio, and a room to store our personal flying gear and pistols.

"Hi, guys." The duty officer greeted us as we entered.

"Put your shit in the PE room back there. Life Support will take your .38s. You guys have the eighteen hundred go tomorrow. And don't worry about flying in the daytime; you'll learn to love it.

"I've got room keys here. It's two to a room. There's a mess hall for chow or you can try the Combined Ranks Club if you want the same food at smaller tables.

"Here's a map of this side of the base, but it's the only one I got so you can't have it. Just memorize where we are and where your hootch is. Other'n that, we'll see you later. Someone will run you up the hill to the main area."

We found wooden pegs for hanging our flight gear, handed over our guns, and got in one of the big vans we called bread trucks for the ride to our quarters. Turning up the hill from the flight line area, we passed sentry positions that blocked each exit into the aircraft parking areas. Abandoned blockhouses, cement mementos of French colonial days, squatted at road intersections. Vast cement-walled ditches lay on each side of the street. They were designed to carry off the monsoon rains without erosion, but now they were dusty and bleached white in the sun. Two Vietnamese soldiers on buzzing motor bikes passed our van from behind, one on either side, unworried by oncoming traffic.

The driver stopped in front of a long, white painted barracks. This was the officers' quarters. The mess hall was just across the street. From inside the mess hall, screaming oriental voices blended with the clamor of pots and pans. Someone was chopping something with long regular strokes; the sound of the cleaver was a repetitive dull thud. Unidentifiable food odors drifted out to mix with motorbike exhaust and diesel fumes.

We grabbed our bags, the driver saluted, and then the van was moving again, surrounding us with a dusty cloud as it hauled the enlisted crewmembers to an identical building further up the hill.

"Well, men, here's home," Terry said. "Now you know why they call NKP the country club." The meal at the mess hall that night was everything I expected.

***

We showed early for mission briefing. We needed intelligence on enemy locations and activities. Unfortunately, there seemed to be too little information and too much enemy. The bad guys, in this invasion, included the whole North Vietnamese Army. These NVA regulars, augmented by the Viet Cong and NVA troops already in the south, had kicked off attacks in three main regions.

To the north, in Military Region I, Quang Tri and Hue had been captured or besieged. The South Vietnamese forces had been pushed back or were locked into isolated pockets. Many units had simply laid down their arms and melted into the fleeing populace. Highway One, known as the "Street Without Joy," and other routes away from the active combat were filled with refugees. The NVA fired with enthusiasm on the packed road to increase confusion and panic. The enemy had 40,000 men in this area along with tanks, long range artillery and wire guided anti-tank rockets. They even moved SA-2 surface to air missiles south of the DMZ, along with radar guided self-propelled triple-A pieces.

Further south, in Military Region II, 20,000 invaders had crossed into South Vietnam from the tri-border area of Laos and Cambodia, hoping to take the important highland province towns of Pleiku and Kontum. North of Saigon, in MR III, another three communist divisions had attacked from Cambodia. After some smaller attacks around Tay Ninh City, the real thrust burst out of the jutting Parrot's Beak region where the Cambodian border cut sharply east into Vietnam. The targets were Loc Ninh and An Loc and their small airstrips. After fierce fighting, Loc

Ninh had fallen. An Loc was now surrounded and cut off, and the defenders lived under constant, heavy artillery and rocket fire. An Loc was only 40 miles up "Thunder Road," highway 13, from Saigon.

In each of these areas, a few American advisers were on the ground with the South Vietnamese forces. They were doing their best to rally their counterparts and organize defenses, but the only real hope to stop the NVA lay with air power. There were more than enough enemy targets to go around.

"Well, there you have it," said the young intelligence officer who briefed us. "I have the call signs and radio frequencies for some of the advisors on the ground in the various areas. I don't know how many of them are still alive and talking by now, but it's the best I've got. You can get more information when you're airborne and contact "ABCCC."

ABCCC was the airborne command center and would have the most current hot spots.

"Just be ready for anything when you take off. I don't have a clue where you'll be used. Any questions?"

"Yeah," Rod spoke up. "Where's Peppermint Patty?"

"Good Luck," the intel briefer said, grinning.

***

Take off was normal. We had a full load of cannon and mini-gun ammo, and enough gas for three or four hours. As things turned out, we should have taken our toothbrushes. When we rolled down the runway it wasn't dark yet, but it was getting there. We had an easy time finding the stretch of road where we were cleared to do a wet boresight for our cannon. Along the road were some burned out hulks of trucks that had been knocked out earlier in the fighting. After a few off-target bursts and corrective computer tweaks, we put more holes in the trucks, then contacted ABCCC, callsign Moonbeam, on the radio and asked where he could use us the most.

"Stinger 51, Moonbeam. If you got the gas, we sure could use you on some targets up toward Kontum. There's some pretty heavy fighting going on now, and we don't have anything available for after dark."

"Moonbeam, Stinger 51. This ain't Texas; it's just a little ol' country. We'll be up there, chop, chop. How about passing us some target coordinates and contact frequencies so we'll be ready when we get there."

"Roger, Stinger. Wilco. Standby for coordinates." Moonbeam began to read a series of map coordinates which Rod copied and plotted on his large navigation map. Then he selected the detailed map numbers he would need and called them down to me.

Next to the NOS position, there was a deep wooden box that we used as a step to climb from the cargo compartment floor to the cockpit entrance about four feet above. Inside the box were ammo cans filled with maps of Laos, Cambodia and South Vietnam. These maps were borrowed from the army and were so detailed that, often, even individual buildings were depicted. The maps were covered with one hundred meter square grids. Using these maps, we could locate the target coordinates within ten meters on the ground.

I dug into the map box, pulled the right numbers, and passed them up to where the FLIR's arm reached from under the bullet-proof curtain. A moment later, one map was passed back, with pencil markings depicting target and friendly troop locations.

"Better take a look now, NOS, before it gets too dark. It's likely things will have changed by the time we get there, but at least this will give you a ball-park estimate of where the bad guys are."

I did my best to memorize the positions drawn on the map and relate them to terrain features I thought I would be able to see in the dark. Then I passed the map back up to the FLIR.

When I looked outside again, I realized the sun had set and all light had faded, except a soft orange glow in the west.

Everywhere across the dark surface of Vietnam, fires burned. Coming in with the air through the open NOS door, the smells of burning rubber and wood were strong and identifiable. Artillery barrages impacted with quick sparks that sometimes grew into flames. Some of the artillery was friendly, and with the help of our flight controlling agencies, Rod was able to plot the impact and origin points to make sure we didn't fly through our own fire. Like all the other aircraft, we took our chances with the enemy fire.

"Okay, crew, Nav. Approaching the target area. FLIR, pick a holding point and we'll contact the ground guy."

As we rolled into an orbit on FLIR guidance, Rod came up on the assigned frequency. "Yankee Four Bravo. Yankee Four Bravo, This is Stinger 51."

"Stinger 51, this IS Yankee Four, Bravo." The nasal voice emphasized the word "is." He was unmistakably American, but Rod used the coded challenge and response to verify his identity.

"Stinger 51, this IS Yankee Four Bravo. I understand you're here to put some ordnance on these Gomers for us. How much play time do you have and what type aircraft are you? Over."

"Four Bravo, Stinger. We have about one point five hours and we are an AC-119 gunship. Over."

"Stinger 51, this IS Yankee Four Bravo. Understand one point five hours playtime. What direction will you make your run-in from? Over."

I was beginning to realize two things. Number one, the Army was a lot more formal on the radios than we were; the guy was already starting to get on my nerves. Number two, he had no clue what an AC-119 gunship was. Being Army, he probably thought we were an Air Force helicopter, hiding somewhere over the horizon where no one could hear the whup, whup, whup of rotor blades.

Our navigator apparently felt the same way. "Four Bravo, Stinger. We are a fixed wing gunship; our guns stick out the side and we shoot from a circle around the target. We got miniguns and 20 mike mike. We can also give you flares. Now, where would you like us to work? Over."

Four Bravo caught on quickly. The 20mm cannon, in particular, could do him some good. "Stinger 51, this IS Yankee Four Bravo. Most of our troops are holed up in bunkers in the main compound. I do have some small two man outposts out, but I'll keep you away from them. We've been taking mortar and small arms fire from the hill to our November. The bad guys are dug in on top and on the sierra side.

"There is also a mortar set up along the blue line to our whiskey. We tried to take it out, but it's got heavy machine gun support. We been expecting an attack on the compound tonight. If you can take out their fire support, they might think twice about that. Over."

Four Bravo passed coordinates for his exact location and the approximate location of the enemy mortars and machine guns. Rod located them on the map. When Four Bravo used the words November and whiskey, he meant the directions north and west. Blue line referred to a stream. They were drawn in blue colors on maps and charts. The target description tallied from the map I'd looked at earlier. We rolled out of the orbit inbound toward him, and told him that we were on the way and would be there in minutes.

I could have pinpointed his compound without a map. Every thirty seconds a mortar round would splash down, making a large flash on target. Machinegun tracers licked out from the compound toward a small hill. The tracers splashed against the hill in a pool of red. Red ricochets detached themselves and bounded in all directions from the hillside. Several enemy machine guns answered from the hill, hosing the compound. From the crest of the hill I caught the vertical pinpoint of light that was a mortar muzzle flash. There would be others on the back side of the hill, where they were protected from direct fire, but could lob shells over the crest toward the friendlies holed up in their bunkers.

"Okay, crew, Pilot. It's time to go to work."

We took up an orbit over Yankee Four Bravo's compound and Rod confirmed with him the location of all the South Vietnamese positions. The bad guys on the hill hadn't yet gotten the message that the cavalry had arrived to save the good guys. They blazed away with as much gusto as ever and ignored us as we droned overhead. Apparently, they didn't know any more about us than Yankee Four Bravo had.

"NOS, Nav. You got anything to shoot out there?" "That's affirm, Nav. Plenty of muzzle flashes, all over that hill. I think I've spotted all the machineguns and I believe one of the mortars is right on the crest of the hill."

"Okay, we'll go after the mortar first. I think we should use the miniguns first, while we feel things out. "Pilot, take NOS guidance, the target is on top of an isolated hill. Our firing altitude will be 4,800 feet."

Rod quickly finished the target briefing, adding that if we took hits, we should go feet wet, which meant east over the ocean.

I held the top of the hill as Terry came on the interphone, "Comin' to you, NOS."

The familiar loud buzz of the minigun drowned out all other sounds. The tracers fell away from the side of the airplane like water poured from a bucket. No single tracer was distinguishable in that stream, yet between each one, there were four more slugs that weren't tracers.

This time, we were firing the aft mini, and the NOS was not blinded by the flare. I could see the tracers arcing down in a long curve, then burning out before they hit the ground. The tracer burn-out was deceptive. From our moving plane, the trajectory of the tracers always appeared to be curving, aimed high and short of the target. But the bullets continued their journey to the target after their incendiary trail had faded.

We fired armor piercing slugs in the miniguns. They were not explosive, but occasionally we could see the sparks as the bullets struck metal or other hard surfaces. This time there were no sparks. We fired at the mortar position again, and again there was no reaction. The mortar, however, had ceased fire.

At the Nav's direction, we shifted fire to the machine gun positions, one at a time, and either destroyed them or ran the gunners into hiding. There may have been return fire at our gunship, but if so, it was only small arms fire and went unnoticed. Gradually, the incoming fire slacked off and we were running short of targets. We dropped flares around the hills surrounding the compound, and the Army scouted outside the wire for bad guys, but it looked as if any planned enemy attack had been postponed.

69

When we had remained on station with Yankee Four Bravo for an hour and a half, the pilot and Nav held a quick consultation and decided that we might be able to extend our usefulness by refueling at some closer base. Quick coordination with Moonbeam set us up for a turn around at Pleiku, just down the road. With Pleiku closer at hand than Bien Hoa, we were able to extend our time over the target area. We hung around but the fireworks were over. When we reached minimum fuel, we headed for Pleiku.

While we had been busy at the compound, a belt of heavy storms was growing to our South. We were in them almost immediately when we turned toward the base. The turbulence was jarring and the old airplane creaked and groaned as it stumbled from one downdraft to the next updraft.

I sat down in the electric NOS seat and strapped myself in. The seat was comfortable and you could run it up and down to adjust sitting height with a switch on the NOS grips, but no one ever sat down in combat. Sitting down seemed to limit the field of view and, in any case, was not considered Macho. All real NOSes stood in the door.

The thunderstorms blasted away the night with lightning and thunder and drowned out the engine noise. Every time the plane tossed and swayed, buckets of rain sloshed into the open doors in the cargo compartment. My flight suit was soaked to the waist and water squelched in my jungle boots.

Around the propeller hub spinning outside my door, a purple flickering glow began to form. It grew in size and brightness until the spinning hub was radiating blue fire up each blade of the propeller. The prop seemed to be one huge fan of crackling Saint Elmo's Fire. Even when the brightest lightning bolts flashed from cloud to cloud, that beautiful phenomenon was visible.

When we finally punched through the ring of thunder bumpers into regular murky cloud, the purple fire was gone as quickly as it had appeared.

We were still in the soup on our approach, and Pleiku was ringed with hills, so Rod set up his radar to direct us down to the runway. He was successful in preventing our crashing into the terrain, but when we finally broke out of the weather, the runway was almost under the left wing, and Terry had to drop the wing and sideslip that 50,000 pound monster onto the concrete strip.

When the airplane taxied to a parking spot, and the engines were finally shut down, we were all soaked. Those of us in the cargo compartment were drenched with rain and those up front were soaked with sweat from the hair-raising thunderstorm penetration and landing approach. The concrete felt unbelievably good beneath our boots. As we gathered beneath the tail, a jeep with two Air Force officers rolled to a stop.

The two captains got out, introduced themselves as part of a forward air control unit, and hospitably offered to share all the resources available. The offer was certainly well meant, but the resources were meager. The captains said there were only about fifty Americans on base and they were living on C-rations and water. But they did have what we needed, airplane gas and 7.62mm mini-gun ammunition.

We held a short planning session. The pilot, co-pilot, Nav and FLIR went with the two captains to check the intel situation and try to contact our operations people back in Bien Hoa. The gunners and I.0. went to dig up ammunition. The flight engineer headed off to arrange refueling. The junior officer, Lieutenant Barbee, was to guard the airplane. Pleiku had received frequent mortar and rocket attacks and the bad guys were known to be in the nearby hills. There was not much that I could do about that with my revolver, but I might be able to prevent vandalism and theft.

After what seemed like a long time the rest of the crew appeared, bringing ammunition and a case of C-rations. Shortly, we were airborne again, feeling fortunate to be away before a rocket or mortar attack could damage our aircraft and strand us at Pleiku. It was almost dawn when we turned north again and contacted Hillsboro, the daytime Airborne Command Post, for instructions.

"Stinger 51, Welcome back. Heard you guys did a good job last night. What have you got aboard that can stop tanks?'

"Hillsboro, Stinger 51. Thanks for the good words." Rod sounded pleased. "As far as tanks go, all we got is 20 mike mike. Works on light tanks but probably not T-54s. Make their ears ring, though. What have you got for us?"

"Stinger, Hillsboro. There's a firebase north of Kontum that's lost its own tanks and now the Gomers are in 'em. They want Air to knock out the tanks. You go on up and help them out."

When Hillsboro passed us the new coordinates and frequencies, we turned toward the firebase and I dug the correct maps out of the ammo can. Within twenty minutes, we were in orbit around the firebase and talking to an American adviser on the ground.

"Roger, Stinger. This is Echo Six. We had an Arc Light supposed to come in pretty close last evening. My colleagues here left three M-48 tanks outside the wire. The Arc Light didn't happen and when they went to get back in the tanks, the bad guys had already climbed in.

"The tanks are still out there, but we can't get the bad guys out. There are a bunch of NVA dug in around the tanks, too. I guess the best thing is to destroy the tanks. You got anything to do that? Over."

I didn't blame the ARVN for wanting to get out of the way of an Arc Light, because it was pure hell on the ground. An Arc Light was a B-52 strike. They usually flew in cells of three aircraft, and each airplane carried 104 big bombs.

They flew and released the bombs at such high altitude that the only warning the enemy had was the first stick of bombs exploding. The result was three very long strings of craters and a lot of new match sticks where jungle used to be. Any monkey or human caught under an Arc Light would be reduced to the fleshy equivalent of those match sticks.

While I wondered why the South Vietnamese troops hadn't just driven the tanks closer to the firebase, Terry answered the advisor from the pilot's seat.

"Echo Six, Stinger. All we have is 20 mike mike. We can get the guys around the tanks but the ones inside are probably pretty safe. Will that help any? Over."

"Stinger 51, Echo Six. That's affirmative. If you can do that, I'll get some of the little people to go down the hill and knock out the tanks with LAWs."

It seemed a waste to have to destroy three of our own tanks when we desperately needed armor. But I understood how the troops would feel with the things in enemy hands and parked just down the road. I sympathized with any soldiers who were going down the hill to attack those tanks with a Light Anti-tank Weapon. These LAW rockets were effective against some armored vehicles if fired from relatively short range.

Getting close enough to fire one could be dangerous and exciting. If the tanks were supported by infantry dug in nearby, it could be almost impossible to get close enough.

"NOS, Nav. Have you got the tanks?"

The guy on the ground had given us some complicated directions to locate the tanks. I thought they were probably hidden under trees or camouflage, because they certainly weren't obvious. Rod called back and the ARVN advisor explained that the tanks were parked right out in the open, in the midst of a network of trails.

The light amplification capabilities of the NOS were useless in the day, because the bright sunlight made the automatic protective iris close down to prevent overload and the entire thing went blank. For daytime use, the NOS had a little auxiliary three power scope mounted above the main tube. Using this little telescope was just about as effective as looking through a cardboard toilet paper roll. It did have aiming crosshairs if you could find a target, but that was as far as the magic went.

I waved the NOS around, tracking little trails outside the firebase until I was dizzy, but those tanks were as good as invisible. No wonder the South Vietnamese lost them, I thought. They probably couldn't find them again.

The FLIR couldn't find them either. That was because the FLIR was broken on this airplane. After another five minutes of fruitless orbiting, everyone, including the Army guy on the ground, was becoming frustrated. Finally, I stowed the NOS, reached into my nylon helmet bag, and pulled out the pride and joy of my Base Exchange purchases, a pair of nine power Bushnell Binoculars. All my life, I'd wanted good binoculars. Now I had them and it was time to put them to the test.

I pointed the binoculars at the dusty scene below, adjusted the focus, and ... Eureka! there was a tank, big as life and more than twice as ugly. The damn thing was just sitting there, a green painted rectangle of steel and cannon barrel, surrounded by empty ammo crates, old oil drums, discarded packing paper and other trash. Near it, just as exposed, sat two more tanks. I dropped the binoculars to hang on the strap around my neck and looked out the NOS door with unaided eyes. Now that I knew where to look, the tanks were there in plain sight, sitting on a little rise, surrounded by trash.

"Nav, NOS. Why didn't that grunt just tell us the damn things were parked in the stupid garbage dump. I've got all of them spotted now." I was embarrassed to have taken so long to find them, but was consoled that no one else on our crew could see them either.

"Echo Six, Stinger. We've got the tanks now. We're going to put down a marking burst with our twenties. We'll hit the tanks, but don't expect too much. Use our marking bursts to direct our fire to wherever the troops are dug in."

"Stinger 51, Echo Six. Wilco. My little people are ready to move out now, under your fire cover. Let her rip."

"Okay, NOS, Pilot. Pick a tank, I'm into the sight. Comin' to you."

I settled the little telescope's crosshairs on the first tank I'd seen and held them steady behind the tank turret, over what I hoped was the engine compartment. In seconds, the Vulcan's barrels spun, spitting out 2,500 rounds per minute. The roar did not seem as loud in the daylight as it had at night.

Around the tank, a whirling dust devil sprang up, bright lights flickering within the cloud. High explosive and armor piercing-incendiary cannon rounds blanketed the target. Terry came off the trigger and I raised the binoculars to evaluate the damage.

75

The dust was drifting away and settling, but a peculiar gray sheen of smoke seemed to lift thinly from the target.

"Pilot, NOS. Hits all over the tank. I think he's smoking."

Hoots of derision came over the interphone. Probably just the dust," Terry said.

"NOS, Nav. I don't think our twenties are going to hurt that tank very much. The armor's too thick."

"Stinger 51, Echo Six. Great shooting. Keep it up. My guys will be in position to attack in five mikes. Then I'll move you around the infantry positions."

I released the binoculars and squinted again through the small telescope. As the crosshairs fixed on the tank, a sudden gush of flame leaped through the turret hatch. In an instant, the entire tank was a furnace of yellow and red. Black smoke begin its climb above the pyre.

"Target's blown up," I said.

"The tank's exploded," Terry confirmed.

The airplane tilted in its orbit as every crewmember rushed to openings on the airplane's left side to observe the miracle. Velcro straps on the bulletproof curtain ripped open as both the Nav and FLIR scrambled to the cockpit side windows.

"Damn sure has," said the FLIR.

Only Jimmy, the copilot, couldn't leave his position to view the destruction. Terry rolled the left wing steeply down until Jimmy was able to see the flames out the left side.

"Way to go, Stinger!" called Echo six. "The bad guys are jumping out of the other tanks and running for the trees. Shift your fire to the north!"

"NOS, I'm into the sight. Target the tree line to the north. Gunners give me number one mini and number one twenty."

"Hold on, pilot. Nav, NOS, what's our heading?" I needed to figure out which way was north.

Rod quickly responded and I pointed the NOS at a point in the north edge of the tree line surrounding the garbage dump. Since no troops were visible, I picked a single tree as aim point.

"Ready, NOS? Comin' to you."

The first burst of cannon shells splintered the tree at the center of the crosshairs. Terry stepped gently on the rudders and the rain of fire walked laterally along the edge of the trees. A movement of the yoke lifted the wing and sent long bursts deeper into the jungle around my aim point. The bright flashes of exploding cannon shells were everywhere in the target area.

"Stinger, Echo Six. They're shooting at you."

"Roger that, Echo Six. No sweat." Terry was getting carried away. We probably would never see the flashes from the rifles and AK-47s fired at us, unless we were looking directly at the muzzle when the gun fired or unless the enemy used some type of small arms tracer bullets.

As Terry paused between bursts of firing, I pulled the NOS crosshairs back down to where the other two tanks were still sitting empty and untouched in the garbage dump. The next burst of fire sprayed across both. This time, only the dust clouds rose. No fires. I was disappointed. I was eager and determined to kill more tanks.

"Move the fire back into the trees, NOS," the Nav reminded me. The real target was enemy troops, not the now vacant tanks. The South Vietnamese could have the two tanks that were left, simply by climbing back in. The bad guys were running for it. We emptied our two cannon into the jungle. As we moved our fire farther and farther from the friendly compound, Rod cut the computers out of the system and Terry fired the guns manually, with all four miniguns on line, hosing the jungle with wavering lines of tracer. When we had expended all our ammunition, Rod called the American adviser on the ground to say goodbye.

"Echo Six, Stinger 51. We're Winchester now and we're heading back to reload. Do you think you'll need us again? Over."

"Stinger 51, this Echo Six. AAh, that's a negative. I think we'll be okay for a while here. I'm gonna have the little people do a full BDA, but from what I can see now, I give you at least 75 KBA. Good work. We appreciate it. We'll forward you more info when we get it. Good day. Echo Six, Out."

"And, over and out to you, Echo Six." Rod switched frequencies.

We rolled out of the orbit and headed back toward Pleiku for more fuel and ammo, discussing the mission results against the tanks and troops. The information Echo Six passed to us meant that we had been effective in producing enemy casualties. For us, BDA was a term meaning Bomb Damage Assessment and KBA was shorthand for Killed By Air.

This time, the approach to Pleiku was in daylight and fair weather. The base looked much more friendly in the sunshine, but the refugees were still flooding the ramp and the same tiny fuel truck was still shuttling back and forth. The only ammo available was 7.62mm so we took enough to reload the miniguns and took off for our third mission.

This time, when we contacted the airborne command post, we were sent to a holding pattern to await developments. There seemed to be plenty of tactical air power around us and airplanes were waiting in line to deliver their ordnance. After an hour of boring holes in the sky, we were released and told to head back to Bien Hoa. On the way, a B-52 Arc Light strike raised hell and dust near us.

Warnings of these strikes were passed a few minutes in advance, over Guard, the emergency channel, to allow all other aircraft to boogie out of their target area. As I watched the three long sticks of bombs walk across the jungle, I was glad I was not under all those exploding trees. I thought how happy I was to fly, rather than endure life as a ground pounding, footslogging Army guy.

We landed at Bien Hoa almost twenty-four hours after our original takeoff. We were tired, smelly and hungry, but as usual, the paperwork came first. Terry raised a fuss when the Intel folks refused to allow us one tank destroyed and two tanks captured. Finally, we were given credit for one tank destroyed and two tanks damaged.

We walked out of the operations shack at twilight. We were already in the bread truck when the detachment commander hustled out to tell us that some other crew was taking our early morning go. Because of our marathon mission, we were being given the next day off. I was a little disappointed. A day off sounded nice, but Bien Hoa's recreational facilities were limited at this stage of the game.

That night, Jimmy and I found a small bar tucked away inside one of the many hootches near our barracks. It was filled with men in various stage of drunkenness. We joined a group of men in flight suits at the bar. Marine, Army and Air Force enlisted men and officers mingled at tables and in the aisles between, each trying to talk above the general hubbub.

Next to me, a young Army Warrant Officer, with helicopter pilot's wings printed on his flight suit name tag, was quoting Shakespeare. His fingers curved around the top part of a white skull, held inverted like a cup. Flourishing the skull expansively, he slopped beer on the scarred bar top. He paused, peered owlishly at the skull, and frowned. Then in a toasting motion, he raised his arm.

"Alas, poor Nguyen, I knew him well," he said, taking a sip. When he moved the skull lower, I glanced inside. Tiny strips of tissue, anchored to the bone inside, floated in the swirling beer. The skull seemed small, perhaps chimpanzee size. I certainly hoped that it was from an unlucky monkey. Glancing at Jimmy, I nodded and we moved further down the bar to finish our beers. One beer was enough, and we headed back to the hootch and our bunks.

***

When we showed up for the next mission, the crew was still tired and looked it, despite the extra rest we'd had. Most of us, instead of snoozing around the barracks, had come down to the operations shack to help out the crews that had been on the flying schedule.

The intel briefer gave us the same old news. The enemy forces were still moving forward in most areas. Civilian refugees were still being shelled as they fled down the major highways, and An Loc was still encircled. Bad guys had fought their way in and occupied a large part of the town. All was chaos and confusion. The only thing the briefer knew for sure was that, this afternoon, our mission was scheduled in support of An Loc.

The Escape and Evasion part of the briefing did not cheer us. The NVA had approximately thirty thousand troops in the region, most of them within shooting distance of An Loc. There were accurate reports of triple-A guns up to 23mm size and unconfirmed rumors of larger ones.

Should we take hits and have to bailout, the best place was over water. It was a long way to the coast, but the further we were able to get to the east, the better off we were.

When the Intel and weather briefings were done, we held a short crew briefing. By now, we knew one another well enough that we briefed most of our procedures as "standard." In the pilot's briefing, Terry asked us all to back him up. "If I prang it in today, it'll be because I'm so tired. You better keep an eye on me as well as the bad guys."

When we reached the airplane, ground crewmen were still loading the guns and flares. Everyone pitched in with the gunners, cranking Vulcan rounds into the big drum magazines which shunted the ammunition along a linkless feed belt into the cannon's revolving barrels.

As I took a break outside before engine start, I noticed the FLIR, Lt. Colonel Taschiologlou, snap a picture of me as I leaned against one of our plane's big tires. There must be at least ten or eleven cameras among the ten men on our crew, I thought. We're a real team of war correspondents.

The takeoff was normal. A quick turn out of the traffic pattern, point the nose to the north, and we were on our way to An Loc, straight up Thunder Road and only forty miles away.

We climbed to 3,500 feet and leveled off. The hot sun pounded the jungle below and the deep green of the trees was bright and hard in its glare. Only columns of rising smoke and dust reduced the visibility. It was a great day for flying. After checking in with the airborne command post, we found a spot for our wet boresight and tweaked the guns. Moments later we were threading our way through the crowded sky over the town. Smoke and dust created a low haze over which FACs, gunships and fighters prowled, adding their weapons to the destruction below.

We stared in awe at the desolate scene on the ground. From our 3,500 foot altitude, the province capitol looked like a beaver dam after a dynamite explosion. Devastated buildings collapsed into mounds of gray rubble choking the streets. Not a single structure still standing looked capable of housing a human. North Vietnamese tanks stood destroyed and abandoned in the streets. A single military truck moved in an alleyway, bumping over debris and tilting crazily as it climbed piles of rubbish. We didn't know if the truck was friendly or enemy.

Still, we knew some friends existed in the ruins below and they needed help. We broke into the radio chatter as Stinger 41, contacting an American military adviser, on our FM radio. His first target for us was a recoilless rifle that was pouring rounds into the South Vietnamese bunkers. The adviser's calm voice outlined the situation in An Loc.

The friendlies appeared to own about a quarter of the town. The North Vietnamese owned everything else and wanted the whole mess. They were busy using their big guns, dropping a continuous artillery barrage on the friendly section of town.

A rain of artillery bursts kicked up dust and smoke and turned what looked like matchsticks into smaller toothpicks. It was already too late to wonder if that arty was coming down through our orbit.

Our most immediate concern was that recoilless rifle, but the ground fire that zipped and snapped around the plane was becoming bothersome as well. From the Quan Loi airstrip to the north, larger rounds began to search for our altitude.

The small arms fire was so heavy and close to us that, standing in my NOS door, I was beginning to feel like an aiming point for the NVA gunners. I suddenly realized that at our altitude we were a great target. The NVA probably didn't get many daylight opportunities to shoot at targets like us. Fat black airplanes, cruising in slow circles above them to give them chance after chance, didn't come their way every day.

For the time being, Terry elected to ignore the ground fire and go after the recoilless rifle below. The target was a tough one. The weapon was concealed somewhere in the heavy trees to the south of town and was blasting into friendlies who occupied an old school building. It was useless to try to see the muzzle blast or back flash in the daylight, so we tried to use the American adviser's estimate of range and bearing from his position to the gun.

The first problem was identifying the friendly position. I had already pulled the correct map. On the map, the town was depicted virtually house by house.

"Find the school house in the south part of town, it's got a flagpole and yellow marking panels out," our American advisor radioed. The background noise of explosions almost drowned his voice.

Standing in the open door behind the NOS, I tried to match the map with the town below. I found the schoolhouse on the map and, with the NOS, pointed the airplane in the right direction. When we approached the schoolhouse, I pointed the NOS in its general direction so Terry could set up an orbit, and pulled out my binoculars. Sure enough, there was the flagpole, but there were no identification panels on the ground, yellow or otherwise.

Rod called the advisor "Stinger 41 has a tally on the schoolhouse, I think. But there aren't any panels out. Over." This time, I was on the radio because the NOS was the primary means of finding these targets and direct communication would be more efficient.

"Sorry, Stinger," the advisor shouted over the sounds of explosions and machineguns. "I'll have some of my guys go put out the panels."

As I keyed the mike to respond, popping noises began to intrude on my end of the radio conversation. Outside my NOS door, beyond the wingtip, a sudden black puff of smoke, with tiny particles like an exploding pepper shaker, burst into being and then was almost instantly gone. With the burst came a popping sound I could easily hear over the sound of the engine and propeller right outside the door.

One of the gunners, hanging over the flare launcher in the right paratroop door, came up on interphone. "Got 37mm triple-A, can't see the tracers in time to call them!"

By flying in daylight, we were losing the scanners' advantage of being able to see and judge the anti-aircraft tracers' accuracy, and to call breaks away from the close ones. The tracers were masked by the sunshine and by the time we saw them, they were already on us. So much for my beautiful day for flying.

We continued around the orbit, trying to straighten out our signals with the ground. When I looked this time, panels were out, but the color wasn't the one we were told to look for. They weren't exactly where they should have been, either. I was sure this was the right location, but the memory of Bald Head and the bad guys monitoring his radios just wouldn't go away. I wasn't about to start shooting until we were sure we had the right target.

Before I could get back to the advisor, the popping noise of the 37mm explosions was back, on the other side of the aircraft, and this time, even louder. With the explosions came a noise like a handful of gravel being tossed on a tar and gravel roof, a tinny rattling sound. We were shedding a rain of shrapnel.

"Stinger, you're taking fire." This from the advisor on the ground.

"Roger that." from Terry.

Terry called down to me, "NOS, he's shooting from outside our orbit. Go back to the scanner and try to pinpoint his position."

To do this, I had to unplug from my interphone cord. I hustled back to the scanner's position with my map. The scanner tried to point out the position from where the gun was firing. No luck. We couldn't orient the map to the terrain we saw outside. By now the gun position had passed out of our view as we continued our orbit.

The problem, essentially, was that the gunner was shooting us in the back. He was firing from outside our orbit and we were only within his range when we were on the side of the orbit closest to him. Since we orbited in left hand turns, almost all of us were facing away from the gun when he fired.

I stayed back with the scanner as we came into his range again. This time he didn't fire. No way to figure out where he was. Smart bastard. I dashed back to my station in the front of the cargo compartment and plugged into the interphone. Terry and Rod were discussing whether we should leave our orbit, regroup and come back in on the target. By the time we came back into view of the schoolyard, the correct panels were out and we were trying to get the range and bearing to the target.

More popping noises, more smoke, more rattling shrapnel on the fuselage. Once more, I unplugged and headed toward the back of the airplane. I leaned out into the slipstream above the scanner. Once more, no joy. The scanner, who was always facing out and away from the center of the orbit, and I, who was always facing toward the center, still couldn't orient ourselves on the map to help place the 37mm. I headed back to the NOS, plugged in and tried to get back into the war. I was beginning to feel like a cuckoo in a German clock; in one window, out another door and back again. Once again Rod and Terry were evaluating our options.

In reality, we were hanging it out pretty far. We had climbed up another thousand feet while I was back at the scanner position, but the shells were still accurate. The 37mm shells were large enough to carve into or through any part of our airplane. They came up in long strings of red tracers, looking slow and dumb, but actually, they were fast and deadly. A single hit in a critical spot, and we would be a four engine fireball.

"Terry, we need to break out, leave the orbit and come back in. That gunner has our range now." Rod spoke with controlled desperation.

"Okay. We'll go around more time and if he comes up on us this time, then we'll leave and come back from a different heading." Terry sounded tired and frustrated, but he was committed to hanging in as long as possible. The mission was going to hell. Terry's words and the subsequent events converted me that day to the religion of pessimism and made of me a fanatic believer in "Famous Last Words."

Of course, the gunner came up on us again. This time three jarring thuds came with the rattling noise of shrapnel. The metal skeleton of the plane transmitted the shivering impacts through the floor to all of us. Someone's voice came calmly over the interphone: "Okay, we're hit, we're hit."

Yogi Bare, our flight engineer, said, "Right jet's gone."

"Right recip's on fire," a third icy voice chimed in. In the cargo compartment, I felt time suddenly begin to slow to a crawl. There was absolutely no panic. The cockpit crew went through the emergency procedures as if they were handling an everyday situation. Rod called an emergency heading to the pilot and began broadcasting a Mayday message on Guard channel.

Because my emergency duty was first aid officer, and it was quickly apparent that no one was injured, I could sit and listen. We called ground advisor and told him we were leaving. It was probably obvious from the trail of smoke and debris that trailed from our right wing.

Behind me an orange glow began to fill the back of the airplane. When I looked toward the aft part of the cargo compartment, I thought we were on fire inside, that perhaps our big flare launcher and its flares were blazing. I grabbed a fire extinguisher, ran as far aft as my interphone cord would stretch and passed the extinguisher to one of the gunners. His expression showed clearly that he believed the old NOS had lost it. Then I realized why. We were not blazing inside the cargo compartment; instead the flames streaming from the right wing extended well beyond the tail or our airplane. Their dancing red reflection filled the plane's interior. The gunner pitched the fire bottle on a seat and I retreated to the NOS position.

My parachute swung from its hook on the bulkhead within easy reach. I looked outside and was surprised to see how terribly low we were. I knew by the interphone conversation that we were losing altitude, but I hadn't realized how much. Below us, individual trees loomed out of the jungle. I moved the NOS to the stowed position, leaned against the bulkhead by my chute and gazed outside.

The cockpit conversation was grim. I began to realize that we might not be landing tonight in the same airplane we took off in this afternoon. When we first were hit, my mind did not allow me to accept the seriousness of the situation. Stuff like this only happened in movies, or in worst case, to some other guy. I guess lieutenants are just slow learners. I pulled my parachute off the hook and clipped it on. Mentally saying goodbye to them, I stowed my binoculars by the seat.

"Illuminator Operator, Pilot. Jettison the flare launcher." I heard a swoosh as compressed air kicked the flare launcher out the aft paratroop door. We would get rid of the flare launcher for two reasons, lighten the aircraft load or prepare an exit for bailout. I hoped that we were only lightening the load.

"Crew, pilot. We can't maintain altitude. Prepare to abandon the aircraft."

Terry was still in control, still calm, struggling to keep the wings level. The aircraft was trying to roll over in the direction of the damaged wing. It took full left rudder and full yoke deflection to the left to maintain a semblance of level flight. If that pressure was released, the right wing would dip, the left wing would come up and that airplane would slow-roll like a sea gull diving for lunch. The only crewmembers lucky enough to get out and use their parachutes would be the ones hurled out by centrifugal force. The recip and jet on the left wing were going full blast and all that power was trying to pull the left wing up and over into that right roll. But without that full power, we would only glide down to the trees below. We had no more altitude to lose.

"Crew, Pilot. Abandon the aircraft! ABANDON THE AIRCRAFT! "

Well, there it was. I would never have believed the number of thoughts that can go through your mind at a time like that. They raced by like little horseflies, zip, zip, zip, one after another:

"Is this real? Naw, can't be. Well, maybe it really is real. Whoops, there goes the first guy, right on out the ole' door. Wow, there goes the next one, right behind him."

"Looks realer and realer." My lips were probably moving as I contemplated all the activity.

In an instant, there were only two guys left in the cargo compartment, me and the illuminator operator, whose duty was jumpmaster. I began walking, slowly, toward the rear of the aircraft. My hands were clasped behind my back in an imitation of nonchalance. The I.O. waved frantically; it was easy to tell he wanted me to hurry up. I walked a little faster. When I got to the door, I looked outside while the I.0., I guess, checked me over for parachute fastenings. The jungle below was a gray-moss green with individual tall trees sticking up over the greenness. Not too far away, a perfect circle of flames was burning in the jungle. I realized that was where our flare launcher had crashed down, spreading white phosphorous among the trees.

I must have gotten some sort of tap from the I.0. telling me my chute harness looked good. I reached up, pulled my helmet visor down, put one hand on the door rim and grabbed the ripcord with the other, and sort of hopped out into the slipstream. As I left the aircraft, I turned my head sideways over my shoulder so the packing board in the chest pack parachute wouldn't break my jaw as it deployed. Numbly, my mind registered the simple thought that raced through it as I leaped, "I hope this thing works." I never saw Ken Brown, the illuminator operator, again.

The C-119 Boxcar had been designed for parachute jumps. As soon as the slipstream caught me, it flipped my feet up so that I was floating down on my back. For an instant, I could see the big black twin booms and horizontal tail surface go by above me as if in a slow motion movie scene. The thought came that there was nothing left to snag my chute, so I pulled the ripcord.

Back in basic survival school, instructors told us to get rid of the ripcord once we pulled it to prevent its being tangled in our gear or flailing us in the wind stream. I had always planned to keep mine for a souvenir, if I was ever unfortunate enough to have to use one. I reasoned that the old gunship wouldn't go fast enough to make ripcord flailing a problem anyway. I will never know whether the instructors were right.

The adrenaline flow must have hit me about the time I left the aircraft. When I yanked that D-ring, the short little cord, handle attached, left my hand at supersonic speed and just kept on going. I would not be surprised if I hold the record for ripcord toss and the thing landed in the South China Sea, miles away.

Things really seemed to be happening in slow motion now. My mind was operating at maximum capacity. I seemed to be falling slowly, drifting down on my back, and watching that parachute just lie there and do nothing. I was beginning to get worried.

Suddenly, there was a kind of "sproooing" noise, and a little puff of cloth leaped out of the chute. The little puff drifted above me in slow motion. "Shouldn't there be more to it than that?" I thought. The cloth began to open with a ripping noise into a little pilot chute that pulls out the real parachute. "So far, so good," I thought.

With a big rip and rush, a mound of multi-colored something popped out of the chute pack and began to stream upward. I shut my eyes. I felt a gentle jar, then bouncing and shaking and flapping. When I opened my eyes, I was floating down toward green jungle, feet first and alive. It was very quiet. "So far, so good." I thought again.

Now that I had time to think, the survival training began to flood back into my mind. My actions came automatically, unbidden. I raised my helmet visor and checked the chute above me. The panels were all okay, nothing was twisted. My eyes fell on the red string stitched lightly on the parachute risers. I pulled the string to modify the chute so that I could control and steer it to some extent.

Pulling down on one parachute riser, I rotated slowly in a circle, looking for a place to land clear of the trees. As I rotated, I saw my blazing airplane, now banking to the right, right wing angling down toward the jungle, starting its final roll. Flames covered the wing and engines and streaked in a long plume past the tail. The right main landing gear was partially extended from the wheel well and large pieces of the wing were flying off in the wake of the flames. On top of the right recip engine, sheet metal had been twisted upright into the airstream by the anti-aircraft shells' impact. The picture was like one of a World War II bomber going down in flames over Germany. It was a sad image, but I didn't have time to worry.

I continued the slow rotation of my chute. I saw no other parachutes, either between me and the ground or in the air near our plane. The only sign of people or activity on the ground was the large ring of vegetation burning around the remains of our jettisoned flare launcher.

As my mind began to clear from the mental shock of bailing out, I found my ears were now functioning normally. I could hear the sound of big guns and probably bombs exploding around An Loc. I was not that far away. I let my eyes follow the sound. I could see the town. I was not that far away at all; not nearly so far away as I would have liked. Machinegun fire sounded even closer than the bombs and artillery. Although I didn't know it, the machineguns were firing at one of our crewmen as he was descending in his parachute.

As I got closer to the jungle, I looked desperately for some place to land and avoid the trees. I didn't want a tree landing because ever since survival school, and the demonstration of a contraption known as the tree lowering device, I was convinced that if I ever had to use it, I would get it twisted and jammed, and while hanging there and trying to get down, some Gomer would come along the trail and casually shoot me as I hung.

The only site I could see that suited my landing requirements was a tiny round clearing. It was surrounded by tall treetops and was back along the track toward the town. I did my best to steer for it. I could see that it was going to be close.

As I neared the treetops, I realized I had no real way to determine my altitude above the trees. I didn't know how tall they were and I remembered reading about World War II paratroopers landing atop tall buildings on D- Day. After their long parachute descent, the buildings didn't seem so tall, so the troopers jumped off and sustained broken bones. If I couldn't judge the altitude, I figured, I'd better get ready for landing. I gave up on getting to the clearing, put my helmet visor back down and assumed the tree landing position I'd learned in our life support training classes. I kept my legs together, toes pointed, covered up all the vulnerable parts that I could and shut my eyes.

Branches brushed my boots. The parachute harness jerked and quivered and I heard a horrendous noise of breaking branches and rattling leaves. The parachute snagged, slipped, jerked free, fell and snagged again. I swung in midair. The only things I could hear were leaves falling around me and bombs, artillery, and small arms fire in the distance.

What worried me most was that my feet weren't touching the ground. The vision of me swinging above the ground while the enemy used me for target practice appeared behind my closed eyelids. That wasn't the way I wanted to die. I opened my eyes. I looked down.

My boots were swinging a few inches above the jungle floor. My trusty old parachute had brought me down to a soft landing in a big tree at the edge of the circular clearing I'd been steering for. I wasn't even dirty. In an eyeblink, I was free of my harness and was standing on the other side of the clearing. It was as if I had levitated from one spot to another.

And then my problems began. I had never realized before that when I was standing in the open NOS door, five thousand feet above the ground without a restraining strap, I was still comfortable because I was in my element. To sit or stand in a flying aircraft, separated from the ground by only a few sheets of aluminum and the swift current of air flowing over the wings, was normal. It was what I did for a living.

Now I had suddenly, somehow, unwillingly, become a Grunt. I felt alone, cut off in bad guy land, and it was just me against thousands of them. I was definitely out of my element.

To say that the most difficult thing to do in this type of situation is to maintain self-control and discipline is an outrageous understatement. Keeping a handle on my emotions when I'd just been inserted, alone, into a whole new world was the most difficult thing I'd ever faced.

The second most difficult thing I had to do was think; think of what to do next and how to survive, because a million thoughts came racing into my mind, riding the adrenaline surge that affected my brain and body. I knew I had to think and act rather than react.

When I paused at the edge of the clearing, it was as much to concentrate on maintaining my composure as to get my bearings. From the direction of the town, the heavy sound of artillery and bombs was continuous. Closer in the jungle, two machineguns, apparently one ours and one of theirs, were dueling.

I fought the tremendous urge to get out my survival radio and scream to anyone who listened that I wanted help, to get me out of there. It was hard to keep my feet from just hauling the rest of my body off in any direction through the jungle, not caring where I was heading, but just running.

Fortunately, the training came through again. I remembered the young Intel briefer telling us to head east, if we had to evade. My mind settled down to figuring out which was east, anyway. Then I remembered. In my survival vest, I had my trusty compass.

When we had first arrived in Thailand, the life support folks had told us we should arrange the equipment in our vests just as we wanted. Being a navigator by trade, I wanted my compass up there where I could find it, in the top left pocket in the front of the vest. What the life support folks hadn't mentioned was that every so often they went through the vests and rearranged all the contents to be in compliance with regulations.

I yanked open the velcro pocket tab and pulled out ... a package of .38 caliber tracer bullets. My compass had been moved! I thought maybe I was confused about where I had put the damned thing. I opened the opposite pocket. I pulled out something else, not my compass. I opened other pockets. All the items I found were tied to the vest by white nylon string. Soon I was festooned with strings all over the front of my vest. I looked like an escapee from a giant spider web.

It was time to take stock. All this feverish searching had consumed about a minute. I was obviously going to have to take the vest apart to find the compass. There must be a better way.

I looked at the sun. It was mid-afternoon. I was sure that the sun still set in the West, even in Vietnam, so I put my back to the sun and headed off through the jungle. The sound of bombs, artillery and machineguns behind me hurried me along.

Each step I took through the jungle growth sounded to me like a Clydesdale tromping on Rice Krispies; Snap, Crackle, Pop. There were dead leaves on the ground and they crunched softly as I hurried along, but with all that adrenaline flowing, each sound was amplified. I could hear like a jackrabbit with a hearing aid. I could have heard a mouse breathe from twenty yards away. I was sure I was making as much noise as a bull elephant and leaving a path like the Oregon Trail. I forced myself to slow down and try to go quietly. It was extremely hard to make myself creep through the jungle, and even going slowly did not seem to decrease the noise. My pulse beat in my ears as loudly as the explosions back at An Loc. I tiptoed on through the jungle.

Thoughts of my family began to intrude. What would my mother do if I didn't make it back? Somehow I realized that if I wanted to see my family again, I had to define my priorities. Survival came first get back alive and the rest would sort itself out later. I was able to squeeze out those unnecessary thoughts and concentrate on the problems facing me now.

Part of jungle survival academics had dealt with the length of time to evade versus the increasing risk of being discovered the longer an evader remained exposed before going into hiding. I began to feel that it was time to find a hiding place.

I looked back the way I had come. I could still see my parachute hanging in the tree. Obviously, my sense of time had accelerated along with my heartbeat. I kept going east, but now I was looking for a good spot to hole up.

Finally, I knew that time was running out. I had to stop creeping and find concealment. Unfortunately, the only spot that promised any cover at all was a big strip of tree bark that had split from its parent tree and fallen to the ground. I stopped beside it and looked back. If I crawled under, I would be hidden from someone following my trail, but if they came toward me from the east, the direction I'd been heading, I would be in plain sight. It didn't seem adequate for my needs, but remembering Mike, the Negrito from Snake School, I crawled under the bark, took a swig of water from my plastic bottle, and tried to become one with the jungle.

I pulled out my .38, set it on the ground beside me, and pulled out one of my survival radios. Cautiously, I raised the telescoping antenna and listened. The Guard channel was very quiet. So far as I could tell, none of my crew had tried to make contact.

In an aircraft with a large crew, each person was assigned, in alphabetic order, an individual call sign for emergencies such as this. I was the fifth man on the call sign list; E was the fifth letter. I was Stinger 41-E, pronounced over the radio as 41 Echo. I waited for someone to come up on the radio. Alpha, Bravo, Charlie and Delta should come up first.

I waited for what seemed like a long time. Then I thought about my last view of our aircraft on its way down. I had seen no other parachutes behind me. I might be the first one on the callsign list that was still alive.

Overhead, a little twin-tailed 0-2 FAC aircraft buzzed around in big circles. I could hear him as he passed directly over my hiding place. I made up my mind.

"Mayday, Mayday, Mayday! This is Stinger Four one echo. Over."

"Okay, Echo, gotcha loud and clear. I'm glad someone's talking down there. This is Covey Two Six." The FAC's voice was reassuring. He had followed our stricken plane from over An Lac and watched as our crew bailed out. He encouraged me to drink some water and find a place to hide. I assured him I had done both. Once I had broken the ice, other crewmembers began to check in with him. He assured each of us that rescue forces had been contacted and the AI-E Skyraiders, using their Search and Rescue call sign of Sandy, were on their way to suppress any enemy ground fire and coordinate the rescue. The Jolly Green Giant rescue helicopters would be right behind them. They would try to get us out of the jungle before dark. If that didn't work, they would come back for us tomorrow, at first light.

Although it sounded like everything was under control, it didn't feel that way. I didn't want to wait out the night in the jungle. That was simply more chance for the bad guys to find us. Back at An Loc, the bombs and guns were still loud. The enemy was around us in force. My imagination was as keen as ever and I pictured the NVA troops skulking through the jungle in search of downed Yankee fliers. I thought I heard barking in the trees behind me. Maybe they were tracking us with dogs. I was instantly alarmed. Probably it was only a bird or monkey, but the barking noises added something new to be concerned about.

Suddenly, the jungle noises were drowned in a tremendous CRAAaacccckk! somewhere in the trees nearby. While lasting only seconds, the echoes of that noise seemed to go on forever. Then from the sky, I heard a deep humming roar that I recognized. The sound was coming from another gunship's Vulcan cannon. Covey 26 had vectored him into our area. The Vulcan's explosive shells were arriving on target before the sound of the gun. I fervently hoped Covey 26 and the gunship knew where each of us was hidden on the ground.

As the minutes passed and the gunship put fire down around us, I began to plan what to do if I was discovered by the enemy. I turned the options over in my mind. How many of them could I handle in a shootout? I could only fire the six bullets in the revolver's cylinder before I needed to reload. What if there were six of them carrying AK-47s? Should I shoot it out and then try to surrender? Might as well shoot it out. After being on the receiving end of all this pounding from the air, the bad guys probably wouldn't be happy with me in any case.

Finally, I heard a new commotion on my survival radio. The Sandy aircraft were showing up and checking in with Covey 26 as Sandy 11 and 12. Then we began a new series of radio transmissions to verify our hiding positions in the jungle. Some of the survivors were changed to a backup radio frequency to lessen confusion during the coming pickup.

There were two Skyraiders in the Sandy flight and they went to work immediately. Through patches in the treetops, I saw them roll in on targets around us and fire rockets.

The noise of the rockets was incredible. They made an evil sizzling, bacon- frying noise as they passed over us to explode with dull thuds on enemy gun positions. I caught glimpses of the Skyraiders on strafing runs, seemingly below the height of the taller trees. Gray gun smoke streamed back from their wing mounted cannon in quick cottony swirls.

The Skyraiders were putting their ordnance in fairly close to our positions. One of our gunners came up on the radio with a question we all wanted to ask, "Sandy 11, this is Stinger 41 Golf. Uh, is there anything going on around us that we should know about?"

"Stinger 41 Golf, just sit tight and don't worry. We'll have you guys out of there in a little."

As the sun fell toward the horizon, the Skyraiders continued to work over the area. The adrenaline was beginning to wear off now, and instead of a steady high, my emotions seemed to peak and fall, and were reflected in my actions. In a fit of glandular bravery, I would get out from under my bark and wave at the

98

planes above. Then, realizing how stupid and exposed I was, I'd zip back under the bark, the cuckoo clock routine again. When a fresh wave of adrenaline would build up, I'd be back outside and waving my gun again.

At last, the HH-53 Jolly Green Giant helicopters checked in. When they announced their altitude as 10,000 feet, I was oddly irritated. I felt that I since I hadn't been at that altitude since I got to Southeast Asia, they should be right down in the treetops with me. I wanted them to get down there and help me out, and immediately.

Eventually the helicopters came down and the Sandy leader began positioning them for the pickup. Because the jungle trees were so high, we were hard to see. There would be some trouble getting the end of the pickup cable down to us at our present locations. After some radio conferences, they were ready to try the pickup.

Sandy 11 circled my area and announced, "The one my left wing is pointing at, pop your smoke."

I was standing now, the tree bark forgotten behind me, with my signal flare in my hand. From some of the earlier radio transmissions, I knew there were other survivors in my area. The rescue pilot was actually circling both me and the FLIR, Lt. Colonel Taschiologlou. For some reason, perhaps RHIP, I decided to let the FLIR go first. I didn't pull the tab to activate the smoke flare.

Neither did the FLIR. The pilot came around again and radioed, this time more firmly, "The one my left wing is pointing at, pop your smoke!"

I thought giving the other guy one chance to go first was enough. I pulled the ring and the thick orange smoke began to fill the little area around me. The FLIR didn't wait this time, either.

Sandy 11 said "Okay, I've got two of you down there. We'll move the chopper between you and both of you go to it."

I ground out the smoking end of my flare in the jungle floor, to avoid starting a fire, just as we had been taught in training. For some reason, I left the flare sticking there in the dirt, thinking if I had need for its unused night end, I could always could come back and get it.

The helicopter moved in on a line between me and where I thought the FLIR was hiding out. I had removed my helmet so I could talk on the hand held survival radio, so now I put it back on and lowered the clear plastic visor. When the helicopter started to hover over the pickup spot, I started off like a fullback, crashing through brush and over small saplings. Noise was the least of my worries now.

The jungle, which before had seemed so open and non-concealing, now was thick. Vines wrapped around my neck and tangled my feet. I dragged the survival radio behind me on its string, disregarding the warning that the antenna was fragile.

The helicopter was just ahead as I crashed through the last ring of brush into a small clearing. The long hoist line was down and I could see the heavy jungle penetrator at its end, hanging just above the ground, waiting for me to fold it down into a seat and ride it out of the jungle.

Suddenly, with a jerk, it began to move upwards and out of the clearing. I looked up: the helicopter was leaving. I yanked off my helmet, slammed it on the ground and yanked the radio to me by its string. The antenna was still in good shape. I held the radio against my ear.

The helicopter pilot was saying something about having a "fire light." This was scary, because I knew that if the Jolly went down, its crew would then become the priority pickup and we would be bumped down the list.

Then things sorted themselves out. Instead of a fire light, the engine overheat light was on. The helicopter was still heavy with fuel and needed to drop some before he could hover without overheating the engines. He pulled away to dump gas.

When the Jolly came around for the second try, it was already dark on the ground and appeared dusky at the helicopter's altitude above the trees. Sandy 11 was leading the chopper in. "Okay, Echo, pop the night end of your flare."

My original flare was back there in the dark jungle, sticking vertically into the dirt. Fortunately, I had another. I ripped it out of the survival vest, and automatically, thanks to my training, found the appropriate end. I pointed it vertically at my nose and, staring directly at the thing, pulled the lanyard.

Instantly my face was pelted with burning sparks. I didn't even feel it. I opened my eyes, held the flare up in the air and waved it around. The damn helicopter wasn't even in sight yet. In fact, when the flare burned out, it still wasn't in sight.

This time I didn't discard the flare. Instead I put it back in its vest pocket and got on the radio, giving vectors to the chopper. At first I could only tell where he was by the sound. Finally, I could see it, coming slowly in my general direction. I gave him directions, "I'm at your one o'clock, half a mile." The chopper altered course.

"Twelve o'clock, 300 yards."

At last I heard the welcome response that he had me visually, and he went into a hover over the tiny clearing. The training that had kept me doing approximately the right thing all day long was still there. I put my helmet back on. When the jungle penetrator came down through the trees, I let it touch the ground to dissipate the static electricity that could kill me. Then I remembered how to unfold the seat on the thing and strap myself on. I gave a huge "thumbs up" gesture and then I was going up faster than a high speed elevator. When I was hoisted into the helicopter, I didn't struggle when the para-rescue sergeant spun me around and pulled me in backwards. As soon as I was unhooked from the hoist, the helicopter banked away, and someone stuck an M- 16 rifle into my hand and pointed me toward an opening. The helicopter crewmember manning a mini-gun at the door was swiveling it wildly, but not firing. I took another opening with the rifle, but as much as I would have liked to, I couldn't see any targets on the ground.

The helicopter then went back and picked up the FLIR, who was shooting mad because he believed the helicopter had left him twice. He had almost been to the little clearing the first time the chopper took off and he was just breaking through the last boundary of brush when I'd been picked up. Both times the helicopter had banked away before he got to it.

We then picked up a third crewmember, Yogi, our flight engineer. Yogi was hoisted up through thick brush and vines and his head was heavily lacerated. He swore that he had been told in survival school to discard his helmet when he reached the ground.

Our helicopter headed for Ton Son Nhut, the major airfield and command center in Saigon. The second helicopter also picked up three survivors. We had no idea what had happened to our other four crewmembers.

When the Jolly Green Giants touched down at Ton Son Nhut, we were greeted by ambulances and cold cans of beer. Climbing down from the chopper, I had the M-16 in one hand and someone shoved a Pabst Blue Ribbon in the other, and then I was blinded by a pinpoint source of bright light.

A CBS news cameraman, who just happened to be handy, was filming us while some reporters rushed forward for interviews. The Air Force major who greeted us pushed us past the reporters, but as I was climbing into the ambulance, one had time to ask me some silly question, like how did I think the war was going. I'm sure my response must have confused the reporter.

"Only ten and half months to go," I answered.

***

When we reached the hospital, all six of us were hustled in to a large examination room where several doctors checked us over carefully for everything from wounds to leeches. We were in remarkably good shape. Yogi's head required a little stitching as did a puncture wound in the back of Lt. Colonel Taschiologlou's leg. The copilot's face had been severely lacerated. His bailout was so close to the ground that his parachute opened as he hit the trees. He was lucky to be alive, and wouldn't have been if the streaming parachute had not snagged on high branches.

Compared to the rest of the guys, I was in pristine condition. I was hardly dirty. The medics hunted around, though, and discovered that the inside of my right ear was caked with dried blood. I guessed that it must have happened sometime during my smashing around in the brush.

The real problem for us survivors, however, was that we were higher than kites. Blood pressure was sky high and we just couldn't sit still. The adrenaline flow had been replenished and now we paced, drank water like camels, and talked even when no one was listening.

Part of our agitation stemmed from worry about our other four crewmates. We each described over and over the last time we had seen each of the missing men. We were missing two men from the cargo compartment. I knew that only Ken Brown, the Illuminator Operator, had been back there when I left the plane. Jimmy, the copilot, believed himself the last man to get out. When Jimmy left the cockpit, Terry was still fighting the controls, holding the airplane steady for the rest of us to bailout. The copilot had not seen Rod, the navigator, or Ken on his way to the rear of the plane to bailout.

Word came from Bien Hoa that Ski, our missing gunner, had been picked up by an Army helicopter. He had been the first one to bailout, and on the way down, an enemy machine gunner did his best make sure Ski didn't land alive. With machinegun tracers licking around his feet, Ski pulled the risers and spilled air from his chute to fall faster. He crashed into a bamboo thicket where the machinegun continued to cut swaths in the brush all around him.

Two Army helicopter pilots, seeing his plight, saved him. One chopper positioned itself between Ski and the gun, and its door gunner opened up on the enemy position. The other chopper crew, unable to land because of the tall brush, heaved a long rope to Ski, who tied it to his chest parachute harness. Then the helicopter yanked him out of the bamboo, with enemy bullets following him as he dangled away beneath the chopper. They hauled him, suspended fifty feet beneath the helicopter, to a place safe enough to set him down and get him inside. Ski was now back at our forward operating location at Bien Hoa. Other than a bad back, Ski was okay.

As the night crept by, the doctors shot us up with sedatives and gave us sleeping pills. They had no more effect than a mosquito bite on an elephant. We couldn't calm down.

When morning finally arrived, we still had not heard any news about our three missing friends. We hoped that Ken and Rod got out. We were sure that Terry had ridden it in.

All that long night, I had visions of what Terry must have seen at the last; the blue line of the horizon as the green jungle grew larger, individual trees reaching closer out of the green, until the black finality of impact. I wondered what he had thought at the last; what he might have said; did he yell or curse? Did it hurt?

After a breakfast we couldn't eat, we boarded another helicopter for the short hop to Bien Hoa. The pilot told us that each of the helicopters that rescued us had taken a single hit. One had a bullet through the fuselage. The one I'd been on had a tire shot flat. The news didn't excite us.

We were greeted warmly at Bien Hoa, not only by our squadron, but by the two Sandy pilots who had led the rescue. We knew them from NKP; they were operating from Bien Hoa in a detachment like ours. When they had heard that a Stinger, a compatriot from Thailand, was down, they pulled out all the stops to get airborne and complete the rescue.

There was still no word from our three guys. We spent the next two days debriefing our experiences to different intelligence and rescue experts, then they put us on a plane back to NKP.

When we arrived, the whole base turned out to greet us. I realized that I was still a "newbie" as everyone else was greeted by old friends while I hardly knew anyone in my own squadron. At least Peppermint Patty gave me a big hug. She and most of the other WAFs were visibly affected by the loss of Terry, whose happy-go-lucky antics had made him a favorite.

That night, at a party, I felt very uncomfortable. In the eyes of my squadron mates, my survival experience now seemed to give me the status of an "old head," but I had no old head friends. I didn't fit in any particular group. I felt alone.

Jimmy, a copilot named Denny and I left the party early, and caught the bus to downtown Nakhon Phanom. At a bar there, we drank into the early morning. Two of us stayed until it was too late to get back on base and took rooms above the bar. I awoke before dawn to the sounds of faint thunder and splashing rain against the window. Storms were rolling south out of Laos, across the Mekong into Thailand. I stepped to the window and gazed out at the river. Half the sky blazed in a constant play of lightning. Behind me, a tiny candle cast shivering shadows across the bed and the bare floor. Far to the east, in a quadrant of sky free of cloud, a stream of red tracers climbed into the sky and winked out in white flashes. "I could write a book about this," I thought. With a sigh, I returned to the bed and blew out the candle.

***

In a few days, we learned that the bodies of all three missing crewmembers had been recovered. The only thing the higher ups would confirm was that Terry had died in the crash. We lieutenants and captains and majors could learn nothing about what happened to Rod and Ken. Rumor had it that they had been captured and executed on the ground.

One of our officers was back at Clark Field in the Philippines when the bodies and their personal equipment were shipped through. Our captain had the additional duty of squadron awards and decorations officer. He felt that if he could see the parachute harnesses that Rod and Ken had worn, he might be able to at least tell if they had had the chance to bail out.

Our captain went to the hospital and talked to the commanding officer, explaining that since Rod and Terry were in the same

106

class, and had been good friends, Rod might have lingered behind in the blazing airplane to help Terry.

Likewise, Ken, who was jumpmaster, might have delayed, waiting for the other two to attempt to bail out. Such heroic actions would be worthy of a suitable posthumous military decoration.

The hospital folks told the captain that there was no problem in looking at the gear, but to come back the following day. When the captain returned in the morning, he was informed that the hospital had contacted our squadron and been told that our guy was not to be allowed to inspect the gear under any circumstances.

And that was that. We put Terry in for the Medal of Honor, but it was downgraded to the Air Force Cross, our second highest award.

Rod Slagle and Ken Brown were posthumously awarded the Distinguished Flying Cross, which they would have received anyway for some of the missions they had flown. All three were awarded the Purple Heart.

A year later, I was visited by an old friend who knew some of the guys in Saigon who handled shipping body bags back home. According to this source, both of our guys had perished at the hands of the enemy after they reached the ground in their parachutes.

At any rate, within a couple of weeks of the shoot-down, official word came down that if aircrews were shot down in South Vietnam, they shouldn't expect to remain alive if captured. In other words, if we couldn't hide, we might as well shoot it out.

I took pains to scrounge another gun, a .45 caliber automatic. It was given to me by a friend I had known back at Texas A&M and who was at Da Nang in another unit.

For the rest of my time in SEA, I carried both guns on every mission. I figured it wouldn't do to be caught short.

BACK IN THE SADDLE

I was itching to fly again, but I wasn't interested in revenge. I was just bored silly. We had rehashed the details of our escape and evasion episode for every official agency that was interested until I was tired of talking about it.

Some of the survivors would never fly again. Ski had loused up his back so badly that he was rotated back to the states. Colonel Taschiologlou, the FLIR, and one enlisted crewman were given ground jobs. The rest of us were scheduled to fly again over Laos, but the schedulers would not let us fly on the same crew. In fact, they wouldn't even designate a new Crew 13. Something about 13 being an unlucky number.

I clamored so loudly that I was the first one back on the flying schedule. My first mission was scheduled with a very experienced senior officer in our unit as pilot. The younger officers had named an informal special award after this gentleman. We called it the "Steel Balls" award and attached his name to it. This distinction was threatened to be awarded at intervals for the crewmember who did the most cautious thing on a combat mission.

When we took off from NKP, the pilot climbed to an altitude that almost made our sensors almost ineffective. If we went any higher, we would have a hard time seeing the ground. At least up here we were relatively protected from small arms fire.

Not long after we crossed into Laos, we hit the Ho Chi Minh trail complex and began poking around for trucks. A slight haze hung in the low valleys below and the jungle looked indistinct and especially dark.

As we crossed one road junction, I saw through the NOS what appeared to be the muzzle flashes from a number of small arms. Tiny streams of bullets cut through the haze layer. I stepped back from the NOS and looked down. I couldn't see anything. When I looked back into the sensor, the ground fire was there. It had to be some enemy unit, probably lying down and spraying their fire straight up toward the sound of our engines.

I had not anticipated how sensitive I would be to someone shooting at me. I had not felt such antagonism a few weeks ago, even when much larger guns were trying to knock us down. I wanted to eliminate those impertinent bastards down there.

"Nav, NOS. We're getting a lot of small arms fire down there. Must be really small stuff cause it's hard to see through the haze without the NOS."

No one was particularly interested in shooting at ground guns, but I was persistent and finally we went into orbit around the muzzle flashes. I picked the center of the area and held it as the pilot maneuvered the airplane into firing position.

"Into the sight NOS. Coming to you."

I squeezed the trigger, but before the pilot could fire, a trail of brilliant red came from the jungle so fast that no one could call a break. The fireball was probably an unguided B-40 anti-tank rocket, but it came so close to the aircraft that my NOS shut down automatically to protect its delicate innards from the glare.

"Out of the sight," said the pilot. "Nav, give me a heading for home plate." With that he terminated the mission and we headed for NKP, still with a good fuel load and plenty of ammunition.

As we turned for home, I noticed my reaction to the sudden shock of that rocket passing by so close to my NOS door. I was glad to take a break. No matter what our pilot's reputation for caution, I could have hugged him for taking us home.

This was the only mission I would fly from Thailand for quite some time. I learned the next morning that I was going back to a Forward Operating Location in Vietnam; this time to our FOL at Da Nang.

***

The trip to Da Nang should have been uneventful. We frequently exchanged aircraft and aircrews between our Vietnamese and Thai bases. One of our birds was heading back to Vietnam with a crew that had been taking advantage of some compensatory time off. I would be the tenth man on the crew. The other two navigators were old Strategic Air Command officers: Ernie, who was a Major, and Scott, a Lieutenant Colonel.

I climbed aboard with the few bags I would need and sat down in the canvas bench seat for takeoff. When we were safely airborne, I climbed into the NOS position, plugged my headset into the intercom system and propped my feet up on the armor plate for the ride.

As we crossed the Mekong into Laos, we climbed to get out of gun range. Visibility was excellent.

Beneath us, I could see the trails we haunted at night. I settled back to enjoy the flight.

Soon, however, an unusual and slightly disturbing conversation began on the intercom. Scott spoke in a puzzled tone, "Ernie, this Tacan position doesn't check out with where we should be. Something's wrong."

"Nah, the Tacan's just screwed up. It's probably got a lock-on error. Let's hold this heading for a little while longer, then we'll cut across straight for Da Nang."

The Tacan was a radio compass that pointed a needle to the radio station selected. It also included a little mileage indicator that read off the distance to the selected station. It sometimes would lock on the station with a 40 degree bearing error. The discussion kept on for the next twenty minutes.

Scott was upset that his radio bearings did not coincide with his chart. Ernie continued to reassure him with complacent chatter. Cigarette smoke drifted down as they chewed over the navigation problem.

The red sun was now setting and our plane's wingtips were outlined with a beautiful orange glow. Below us, dusk crept deeply over the jungle and shadowed the trails. When I leaned slightly forward, I could see a wide spot where a trail or rutted road ran parallel to the banks of a small river. A moving light reflected from the water's surface and there was some type of angular object in the clearing.

Suddenly the entire clearing exploded with an intense flash of white light. The trunk of each tree was outlined in the instant glare. A white- hot tongue of flame leaped directly toward me and seemed to rise almost to our altitude. I flinched back inside the NOS door with my mouth open and watched as high above us a bright explosion flared and faded into a cloud of smoke. Immediately below us, another tongue of flame lanced upward. I jerked my toes off the vertical armor plate and stood up on the small square of armor inside the door.

A second explosion was just as high above us, but seemed much closer to our line of flight. The gun was tracking toward us, his accuracy getting better, and the shells were going right by us with a supersonic crack to explode above.

I found my voice with a squawk. "Triple-A, nine o'clock."

Other voices overrode mine on the intercom as the gunners in back with me leaped to their scanner positions. "Holy Shit. It's a fifty-seven. Break right! Break right!

Another voice, higher pitched, "Maintain right break! He's still shooting!"

For the first time, the pilot came on the interphone, saying, "We're breaking right, coming right, hang on!" Our right wing dipped sharply into the hard turn to the right, and I heard the engines wind up to full power. From my position in the left side of the airplane, I could only see sky. I felt as if I were looking straight up. All I could do was hold on and wait till we rolled out of the turn. Above us, two more flashes and smoke clouds popped into the sky. The break saved us from the second of these. It would have been very close if we had continued straight and level.

It was over in a minute. We had dodged out of his range. The gun had ambushed us, and he had missed a sitting duck. Our aircraft had been slow, low and outlined by the sun, while the gun was hidden in the dusk-filled jungle. We were lucky he wasn't radar controlled. We were just plain lucky.

On the flight deck, Scott and Ernie were raising hell about the gun. Scott was flapping the map. "What the hell is he doing this far south? There shouldn't be a gun that big anywhere around here! Get his coordinates and we'll have the fighters come and blast him. Unfold this map."

Ernie said nothing for a moment and then asked quietly, "What do you mean, unfold the map? The map's not unfolded? Let me see that thing!"

Over the intercom came the noise of rattling paper, followed by heavy breathing. Then Scott said very distinctly, "Pilot, Nav.

Come right, heading 170. Now! We keep up our present heading and we'll cross into North Vietnam above the DMZ."

There was silence on the intercom as the pilot started a long hard turn back to the right. Finally, Ernie keyed his mike, "Our mistake, pilot. No wonder those Tacan bearings didn't make sense. Our map wasn't opened up all the way. We'd crossed most of Laos and were headed directly for North Vietnam."

Once again, we were lucky. If we had made it much further in the direction we had been headed, we would have been in the back yard of Mig fighters, surface to air missiles and radar guided anti-aircraft guns. I spent the rest of the flight to Da Nang sitting on an empty ammo can between the two Navs, looking over their shoulder and very quietly making sure every map and piece of paper they used was unfolded.

***

When we started our let- down for the approach to Da Nang, I got a good look at the darkened valley that soldiers and aviators called Happy Valley. Somewhere in those curving ridgelines were caves that protected a medium size triple-A gun. Every now and then the bad guys would drag the gun out and blast away at some passing airplane.

So far, the Americans had never been able to catch the gun exposed and put it out of action. It remained a nuisance to be avoided when possible.

My introduction to the flying conditions around Da Nang began with the base Air Traffic Controller's first radio call to us. "Stinger 32, report over the bridges. Caution for tracers on final."

Over the twin river bridges that were a favorite traffic pattern reference for the base, we altered our heading toward the final approach heading. I noticed that the controller had not been making idle conversation about the shooting just off base. A full-fledged firefight seemed to be taking place right off the end of the runway.

To make us less of a target, the pilot killed our aircraft's flashing position lights and the red rotating beacon before we turned final. The landing was uneventful. We taxied to a parking spot between the earth-filled walls of a huge metal and concrete revetment and shut the engines down.

A big lieutenant colonel wearing a Stinger flightsuit was waiting for us, a dead cigar clamped in his teeth. I didn't think I'd ever met him, but he seemed to know me.

"Here, Larry. You'll need these," he said as he held out an army style steel helmet and a heavy flak jacket. "Welcome to Rocket City. Don't go out at night without 'em."

The colonel's tag said he was Andy Danielson. I noticed that as he welcomed the rest of the crew home, he never removed his helmet. The ground crew and crew chiefs working around our plane were all wearing flak vests or had them nearby. This was beginning to look like the real war zone. A closer look at my helmet showed a list of dates written in ink. The dates started at the middle front of the helmet and marched single -file up the helmet to the top, and started down the backside. I had the feeling these were rocket attack dates. The last entry was dated only a week earlier. I hoped this meant that the former owner had rotated out of Da Nang. I didn't want to think about the other alternative.

We finished up at the airplane and went into the maintenance hangar to complete the ever present paperwork. Each man who worked in the maintenance and aircraft scheduling area kept his flak jacket and helmet either on top of his desk or under it.

Finally, we climbed into a van and headed around the end of the runway toward Gunfighter Village, the barracks area most of the Stingers called home. We drove slowly around the base perimeter road. Guards with rifles and machineguns occupied sandbagged posts along the outside of the road. Beyond them, the base main fence formed a barbed wire wall. On the other side of the fence, razor-edged barbed wire was staked down under rolled concertina wire. Beyond the wire, the mine field began.

When we pulled up at one of the two-story barracks, I was introduced to my new roommate, Tommy. Tommy was the pilot and aircraft commander of the crew to which I had been assigned. Tommy was a short, cheerful captain. Tommy was always in good humor because in a couple of weeks, he would rotate back to Thailand, and two months later, head back to the States. Tommy was a new first-time father, and he was really itching to finish up his tour and see his son for the first time. Tommy would show me the ropes, not only about flying from Da Nang, but also simply living on the base.

Gunfighter village was named for the 366th Tactical Fighter Wing which flew F-4 Phantoms out of Da Nang. The Stinger crews shared the area with the Gunfighters and the "Bullshit Bomber" crews who flew psychological warfare missions in old EC-47 Gooney Birds.

Gunfighter Village was not attractive, but it was much nicer than many other parts of the installation. It was on the American side of Da Nang at the south end of the sprawling base, and across the runway from the South Vietnamese military area. The much plusher headquarters area of the base was more centrally located, and only a few of the Stinger senior officers lived there.

Our area boasted a small base exchange, with a little Chinese restaurant nearby, a soft ice cream stand, and a little snack bar. This snack bar was known as the "No Hab Kitchen," because no matter what item a customer first asked for, the little Vietnamese waitress invariably responded, "Sorry, no hab." I soon developed a habit of trying to outfox the waitress, by asking first for something I didn't want.

We also had a small movie theater. When we went to an afternoon movie, the doors leading from behind the big screen to the outside were usually opened to ventilate the place before the movie started. As the sunlight illuminated the screen from behind, we laughed as big rats jumped and played between the screen and the open doors, their shadows enlarged to the size of small dogs against the movie screen. I called it the Rodent Review Show.

Our day was never complete without a run to the base exchange and an ice cream snack purchased from the cute Vietnamese girl who worked there. The BX run, as we called the visit to the exchange, was simply a habit, because there was rarely anything new there. The facility was new and spacious, but merchandise was sparse. Most of the things in the electronics section seemed to be special order items that some G.I. had rejected. There were no matching lenses for camera bodies.

The most abundant items seemed to be liquor, canned sauerkraut and various feminine hygiene products. I could understand the liquor; some people considered drinking to be the only recreation available. The sauerkraut had to be there just to make the shelves look full; a regiment of Germans couldn't eat that much kraut in a year. What really had me buffaloed was the huge supply of feminine products. I knew of only a couple of Army nurses on the base. I finally decided that it must be a black market item, although I never saw anyone make a purchase.

***

The first mission with my new crew took us north toward the old imperial capital city of Hue. During the 1968 Tet offensive, hard fighting had been necessary to finally clear the enemy from Hue's old walled citadel. Now, the friendly forces still held the city and the citadel, but conditions were desperate. The NVA had taken Quang Tri, closer to the DMZ, and were bringing tanks and troops south to bring more pressure on Hue's defenders. The South Vietnamese high command had relieved the region's commanding general and replaced him with a hard-fighting general who had participated in the 1968 battle for Hue.

Once again, our intelligence personnel were not at all sure of the NVA's strength or capabilities around Hue. The enemy's anti-aircraft defenses had proven more threatening than anticipated. The NVA had brought a new weapon south with them, a heat seeking anti-aircraft missile known as the SA-7 Strella. It was man-portable, meaning that a single enemy soldier could carry and launch the weapon. Like our FLIR, it carried an infra-red guidance system to home in on the hot metal of aircraft engines and exhausts. We had tried various combinations of decoy flares and maneuvers to defeat the seeker head, but many aircraft were still being lost and damaged by the new weapon. It was especially effective against slow movers like gunships and FACS.

The North Vietnamese forces had not forgotten to bring along their larger anti-aircraft guns. We knew that SA-2 Guideline radar guided missiles had been moved into the DMZ, but we didn't know how far south they might be by now. The bad guys had a formidable array of defenses, and our lack of knowledge on their precise location was to their advantage.

Our crew was tense as we began an orbit north of the city and contacted an American adviser on the ground. He directed us toward an ARVN firebase that had been overrun by the enemy. We were to destroy or disable as much of the abandoned equipment as we could.

When we found the firebase, it seemed as if we had slipped in through a crack in a wall of fire. From hilltops all around us, anti-aircraft fire rose into the sky in sheets. The fire from the closest hilltop was from either a quad-barreled 23mm or else several guns were sitting wheel to wheel. The white tracers surged upward as if from an illuminated fountain. We felt it unbelievably good luck that the guns weren't directed at us but at aircraft at higher altitudes.

Below us, the hilltop was covered with abandoned vehicles and heavy artillery. We put a single Vulcan and a minigun on line and swept the hill and the road leading up it. The secondary explosions were spectacular, and fires spread unchecked across the target. When one gun was empty, we switched to others while we reloaded.

For some reason, none of the AAA guns around us fired in our direction. The NVA in the target area blindly sprayed small arms fire at the sky, but to no effect. Although we couldn't tell for sure, the fire seemed to be from people fleeing the hilltop.

The real excitement came when we had expended all our ammunition and were trying to pick our way back out of the triple-A maze defending the surrounding hills.

When a scanner called "Missile, Missile, Missile!" I watched helplessly as a bright light climbed from a hillside off our left wing. The thing was flickering like a bright star, getting bigger, apparently on a collision course with our gunship. The illuminator operator was punching flares from our launcher and the scanner fired a Very pistol flare at the thing to try to decoy the seeker head. There was no change in the rocket's heading.

The white light continued on course, accelerating, until it passed beneath our aircraft. There was no explosion. It just kept going until it finally curved down and splashed against a bare hillside. No further ground fire was directed at us. We squeezed back through the curtain of triple-A and finally landed at Da Nang just before dawn.

We were never able to identify the rocket we saw that night. The common description of a Strella launch and flight said there was a ground flash as the rocket motor ignited, then the missile appeared as a glowing neon tube, with a slight corkscrew motion as it tracked its target heat source. The SA-7 launches that I observed later fitted this description. Our unknown projectile just didn't have these characteristics.

The missions to destroy abandoned supplies and equipment became common as the communist forces moved closer to Da Nang from the rough jungle country to the west. Hue still held in the North, but the enemy appeared to be trying to cut all the way to the coast south of Da Nang and block the coastal highway. To our southeast, Firebase Ross fell, then Firebase Baldy. Baldy was only 22 miles south of our base. We flew day and night missions to destroy the 155mm artillery the South Vietnamese had left intact at the firebase. What worried us the most was that the NVA might move in their own 130mm guns, which fired accurately for 17 miles. We Stingers held a meeting to discuss the situation. It was clear that our airbase was in jeopardy. If the artillery could reach Da Nang, it might destroy our runway. We might have to evacuate by ship. We set priorities for a possible evacuation. The first and most important thing was to save our stereo equipment. We started to load tape recorders, amplifiers and turntables on our gunships. We flew combat missions and dropped the stuff off at NKP for storage. Then we turned the plane around and flew another combat sortie on the way back to Da Nang. I was sure I had the only miniature refrigerator that ever completed a combat mission.

As the North Vietnamese drew closer to the coast, their rocket attacks and probes of Da Nang's barbed wire defenses became more frequent. Our gunships were kept closer to the base, working in what we called the "rocket belt," to preempt attacks. We were often teamed with Army helicopters from Marble Mountain, a helicopter base just to our south.

To me, these missions usually seemed boring and I missed the action of truck hunting or TICs. But stopping the rockets was a big morale factor at Da Nang.

Each of us had our own early warning indicator for predicting impending rocket attacks. Many relied on the Vietnamese maids and the incense they burned. These Stingers believed that some of the maids knew when the attacks would be launched and burned incense in our quarters to protect the building. The Stingers disagreed on whether the maids wanted to protect the hootch because they liked the Americans or because they would be out of a job if the barracks were blown up.

My special early warning system involved noting what time the cute little ice cream vendor shut down her shack and headed for the gate. This ice cream stand was right across the road from my room and I noticed that some days she closed earlier than others. Deep inside, I was sure there was no correlation between her high-tailing it off the base and the rocket attacks, but I found myself more alert on those days when she closed early.

On the thirteenth of June, she left early. I was scheduled for the midnight mission and was sitting idly on the concrete step outside our barracks when she quickly pulled the shutters over the front of the booth and hurried to the gate leading out of the Gunfighter compound.

That night, Jimmy, my copilot friend, and I headed to the mess hall for a late snack. As we finished and left, Tommy, my crew's pilot, and Denny, our copilot, came in to eat. Jimmy and I talked with them for a moment and then returned to the barracks.

Back in my room, I sprawled on the low bed, reading and waiting for the time to head up to the squadron and mission briefing. Suddenly the walls seemed to compress under the force of an explosion. Instantly, I hit the floor and rolled under the bunk, covering my back with my flak jacket and propping my steel pot over my head. The explosions walked closer, jarring bug spray cans and other junk off the desk. The concussions popped screws from the wall, and a mirror crashed to the floor, shattering. Wow! I thought excitedly. This is really like being in a war movie.

The rocket attack stopped abruptly, and I hustled outside. A fiery orange light flowed over Gunfighter Village from the flight line. A fuel truck and its two Korean drivers had taken a direct hit. The burning fuel's glare lifted the darkness from our end of the base.

The barracks next to ours was occupied by the Bullshit Bomber guys. Halfway up the outside stairway, a body sprawled on its back, headfirst down the steps, inert. I started up the steps three at a time, but two men came out of the upstairs door and beat me to the man.

"I think somebody's hit down there!" one of the men yelled, pointing up the street. "I heard him yell." I doubled back down the steps and headed up the street. I almost stumbled over the body in the shadowed alley intersection. I heard him before I saw him. Before me, a man lay face down, and a long strip of asphalt was already wet with dark blood flowing downhill toward the main street. The man moaned, and his right foot made little scuffling noises as his leg bent, then straightened. When I knelt beside him, the only wound I could see was a small exit wound in the right buttocks, where ripped flesh and flight suit cloth lay open like the petals of a too-old rose. This wound was hardly bleeding; the blood had to be coming from the front of his body.

I didn't want to turn him over. I yelled for help, for someone to bring matches for light, for an ambulance. Everyone in sight was busy back up the street. I rolled the man over on his left side. As I did so, his right arm rolled too, flopping back down limply beside him. It was nearly severed, a few strands of stretched flesh and cloth limply attaching it to his shoulder. A cavity seemed to exist where his arm had joined the body. Blood was running in sheets from the opening and down the front of his uniform. I yelled again for help, but no one seemed to hear. I tore off my flak vest, unzipped my flight suit and yanked off my T-shirt. Wadding it into a ball, I shoved it into the bleeding hole and held it there with as much pressure as I could. As I watched, the white shirt grew dark with blood.

Beside me, a man skidded to a stop. I looked up and saw Gus, the flight engineer on my crew. "Light a match, Gus, so we can see if he's hurt anywhere else." My voice sounded raspy and far away. Gus's lighter flared just as an ambulance slammed to a stop beside us. People with medical kits ran to us and began to work on the injured man. I flopped backward and sat cross-legged as they eased him onto a stretcher and slid him into the ambulance. I think that, in a haze of relief, I told them they could keep the T-shirt.

Gus and I walked back into our barracks and joined an excited group of men recounting their experiences in the attack. Each of us was talked rapidly to anyone else who would listen. Eventually, our voices slowed as we talked ourselves down from the adrenalin high. Then a quiet voice asked, "Where's Tommy?"

Gus and I looked at each other. His face went pale as our eyes locked. We knew where Tommy was then; we just hadn't realized who he was.

Perhaps the darkness had kept us from recognizing a fellow crewmember. I had noticed that the man was wearing a flight suit, but the significance of that hadn't surfaced in my mind. The shock of the sudden realization that Tommy was the injured man was a physical blow that took my breath.

When we flew the midnight mission that night, Steve Meleen, the pilot for the night's first mission, climbed out of his airplane when he landed and flew as the pilot in our plane. Gus and I flew the mission in a daze. Steve was quiet too; he was Tommy's close friend. There was no news when we landed. Tommy had been evacuated to a major hospital by air.

The next morning we received good news. Tommy was going to live. His arm had been amputated, but his chances for recovery looked good. Everyone was cheered by the news.

Two days later, word came that Tommy hadn't made it after all. We were standing in the hall outside my room when we heard. One of Tommy's friends, a captain, began to cry. I felt nothing, no shock, no emotion. I was empty, wooden and hollow inside.

For a long time, I would wonder if perhaps I had done more harm than good with my hasty action to stop Tommy's bleeding. And as long as I was at Da Nang, I always stepped carefully around the faint brown stains on the dusty road to our squadron.

***

June was a bad month for me. Early one afternoon, I sat at a squadron scheduling desk, feet propped on an open drawer, and chair tilted back comfortably. In my lap, I held a copy of the Stars and Stripes newspaper and scanned the daily news of the war to see how we were doing.

Among the stories of battles and rescues, I noticed a small column about an airplane crash far from the combat zone. A C-130 cargo plane had flamed and crashed into the sea near Taiwan as it made practice landings during a routine training flight. There were no survivors; not even all the bodies had been recovered.

Idly, I scanned the list of crewmembers' names who had died. One name stopped my breathing for a moment. John Boehringer was one of those whose body was not recovered. John had been my best friend in Nav School. John and I and our wives had gone everywhere together. The two of us were always in the doghouse together for some breach of etiquette. I thought about our taking our wives to a strip show in Sacramento so that, as Johnny said, maybe they could learn something.

Johnny had stopped by NKP shortly after I had been shot down, but I had been sleeping and he elected not to wake me. I wished that he had. Once again, I imagined what that final plunge toward earth or sea must be like, and what thoughts must pass through a person's mind.

At the time I didn't know the whole story, that my wife had flown to Illinois to visit Lockye Boehringer. They were returning

125

from shopping when they saw the blue Air Force staff car parked in front of Lockye's house.

A military car cruising a civilian neighborhood as the driver looked at house numbers was always a sad omen during the Vietnam War. When the car parked it was a sure sign of tragedy.

A chaplain and an officer were waiting. Both women were upset. Both thought that the bad news would be for Debbie, since they knew that I had been shot down before. Instead, Lockye was the one the officers waited for.

When I heard about it later, I thought how terrible it must be, that, when tragedy is on your doorstep, you pray that it strikes your best friend instead of yourself. And how difficult it must be to share that tragedy with someone, when you are so glad that they, rather than you, are the victim.

The misfortunes of June convinced me that if Debbie could find a way to get to Thailand, she should take advantage of it. She had talked about getting a visa and living there as some other wives did. I had resisted originally, but now my mind had been changed by unhappy events. At the rate things were happening, I thought I should take any opportunity to get to see her.

Debbie was able to get to Thailand and spent five months in Bangkok, working as a substitute teacher in the American School. In those five months, I saw her five times. Twice in Bangkok and three times in NKP. It seemed ironic that when she went to Cambodia to get her visa renewed, I was going to Cambodia at night to destroy trucks and sink sampans.

***

Andy Danielson stopped me in the hall at the squadron building.

"Larry, I need to ask you if you have any reservations about going back down to Bien Hoa, just temporarily. I know you may have some bad memories, and if you want I'll send someone else."

"Colonel, I appreciate your concern. But I don't mind going back at all. I'll be glad to get out of flying these rocket belt missions. I'm so tired of just going around the flagpole, I'd jump at the chance to go anywhere. Thanks for asking."

*　*　*

When I arrived back at Bien Hoa, nothing had changed but our missions. The South Vietnamese had been able to hold on to An Loc while the NVA had expended its people and energy by trying to capture cities. When the NVA assembled enough men and material to mount a major attack, their troop concentrations were pounded from the air. The enemy no longer had the people for massive attacks. The South Vietnamese forces were pushing back, retaking the larger cities. Now the NVA invaders were trying to hold on the countryside they had conquered at such cost.

The Bien Hoa Stingers were flying night missions west into Cambodia, south to the Mekong delta and north into MR II. There were a few truck hunting sorties from Bien Hoa, but the majority of fire missions were in support of troops on the ground. Most of us gained more satisfaction by pulling another American's chestnuts out the fire anyway.

The American advisers on the ground were dedicated to helping the South Vietnamese survive the threat from the North. They risked their lives every day in vile conditions and worked hard to build an effective self-supporting fighting force for our Allies. They were brave and competent. They had our respect and we did our best for them.

"Stinger 36, Alleycat," came the call from the Airborne Command Post.

"Alleycat, Stinger 36. Go," replied "By the Book Bert."

He was on top of things tonight. He ought to be; he was a major with zillions of flying hours. "Stinger, Alleycat. We got a TIC about 30 miles north of Bien Hoa. Need you up there ASAP. Stand by for coordinates, call signs and frequencies."

Bert copied the coordinates, had the copilot check clearance from our artillery fire, and gave the pilot the best heading, while I took one more look down the tree covered canal that emptied into the Mekong. We were looking for boats in the Mekong delta and things had been slow. It sounded like this call might liven things up a little. This would be Bert's first TIC since he had been checked out as Table Nav.

I had been checked out on the FLIR. I didn't have the thousand navigator hours required to qualify as Table Nav, so I had been designated as a sensor instructor and flew with new navigators as the experienced person behind the bulletproof curtain.

Like many of our navigators, Bert had been somehow pried out of Strategic Air Command's heavy bombers and tankers for gunship duty. SAC was a stickler of a Command for regulations, and Bert's adherence to the regs had earned him the moniker of "By the Book Bert" from the rest of the Stingers.

Bert was a detail kind of guy and for our missions, his flight planning ritual bordered on overkill. Since we rarely knew where we would be going until we were airborne, we had plastic covered charts with Tacan bearings and distances already drawn in. When we learned of a target, we plotted it out, gave the pilot the Tacan bearing and DME, which stood for distance measuring equipment, and he piloted us there. Once in the area, we used our sensors to find the precise target. Bert wanted to plan with more detail.

When we did our aircraft preflight at Bien Hoa, the crew climbed in, checked our aircraft equipment as fast as possible, and went up the hill for midnight chow. We figured if the bad guys launched a rocket attack, we would rather be caught in the mess hall than on the flightline.

This was not sufficient flight planning for Bert. After preflight, Bert would remain alone in the aircraft, sitting exposed and surrounded by tons of fuel and ammunition as he flight planned. No one knew what kind of extra flight planning he did, because no one else was going to remain down there with him and find out.

Until one night, when the rocket attack came in while the crew Bert was flying with was at the chow hall. Nothing came close to the dining hall, but when they crawled out from under the tables and looked out the door, flames and big secondary explosions were coming from the flightline area where we parked our gunships.

The detachment commander saw the crew bread trucks outside the dining hall and stopped to count noses before going down to check the damage.

"Everybody okay?" he asked.

"Bert's flying with us," said the NOS.

The commander understood immediately. He turned on his heel and sped out of the mess hall. They all hurried out to the vehicles and followed the commander's car down to the flight line.

Bert was sitting unhurt at the edge of the entrance to a concrete and metal revetment. Beyond the revetment wall, the fire trucks were putting out the final flames from a little Vietnamese F-5 fighter. The rocket had gone right over our airplane and exploded in the next revetment. Bert had rushed out of the gunship at the first warning and was lying on his face exactly on the other side of the revetment wall when the plane went up. He was shaken but flew the mission.

The same crew was on the schedule again the next night. After preflight, they hustled into the bread truck for the trip to midnight chow. "Hello, Bert," said the NOS, as he sat down in the van next to Bert. "Flight planning all done?"

"Yep," answered Bert. Bert never again stayed behind to flight plan, but he never lost his nickname.

He was a likable guy, thorough, and very efficient, and he smoked like a city bus.

To be trapped with Bert behind the heavy felt bulletproof curtain when things were tense was an experience you didn't want to repeat. I had learned from experience. Over a Cambodian road, Bert lit cigarette after cigarette while we fired at trucks and the ground gunners fired back at our muzzle flashes. He would have two or three smokes going at once, and the smoke built up behind the curtain until my eyes filled with tears.

One thing I had learned about the Table Nav position was that once everything was all set up, the Nav still had a lot to do but physically he was pretty much sitting on his hands, and only had to manage and monitor the attack, watch the FLIR track targets, and listen to the whizz and crack of triple-A fire go by. It could be hard on a naturally nervous person. Behind the bulletproof curtain, when the gunship broke away from close anti-aircraft fire, there was nothing to do but watch the altimeter and compass and wait for a hit. At least the FLIR could translate the tension into activity by trying to keep his crosshairs on the target.

Tonight, we probably wouldn't have to worry about big guns, but it sounded pretty bad at the little compound under attack. I hoped Bert wouldn't feel the need for more than one cigarette at a time.

As we entered an orbit over the small compound, we could see that the friendlies were under heavy attack. One side of the walled area was a volcano of mortar and rocket propelled grenade flashes. On the FLIR screen, the explosions blossomed in bright white puffs that quickly faded back to neutral gray. I could easily see the compound wall that ran around the entire area. Inside the wall were orderly rows of buildings or bunkers. The area enclosed by the walls seemed to be about 100 meters square.

Delta Two Tango, an American adviser, gave us a quick lowdown on his situation. As he spoke into the radio, the background noise of rifle and heavier automatic weapons fire was clearly audible. Cries of excited Vietnamese soldiers could be heard in lulls in the firing.

"Stinger, we have bad guys over the fence and in some of our bunkers. We're fighting building to building. We're pretty well bunkered down in here, so we want to bring you in pretty close. We're going to start you off on the wall." Delta Two Tango sounded competent. He also seemed to understand gunship capabilities. Months earlier, prior to the NVA invasion, that was not the case with most of our Army friends.

"Delta Two Tango, Stinger. If we're going to shoot that close, we'll need you to accept responsibility for any short rounds we drop on you. Just give us your initials." Bert sure knew his regulations.

A short round was a weapon's impact on a friendly position. We tape recorded the communications during missions and should our fire injure or kill friendlies, we would need the initials to prove we were cleared to fire. During hot fights, our crews had sometimes fired at bunkers with our miniguns when the good guys were inside and the bad guys were on the outside trying to get in.

Delta Two Tango passed his initials and the exact section along the wall he wanted us to hit. Bert set up the fire control computer, I held the target on the FLIR screen and we fired a long burst of 7.62mm. Behind the felt curtain, the sound of the minigun was remote. We waited for Delta Two Tango to come back with corrections to our aim point.

"Stinger, that was a good burst, but it looked like it was outside the wire. The bad guys are in the first hootch inside the fence where you are firing. If you can see that building, hit it."

"Roger, Delta Two Tango, be advised we can see the buildings. We will hit the fence and the first building inside." Bert was handling the radios well. He was only smoking one cigarette.

We fired two more bursts, one along the fence and one at the building. Targeting looked good on the FLIR.

The bullets should be hitting where the bad guys were.

"Stinger, all those tracers look long from here," Delta Two Tango came back on the radio. "Move it in about a hundred meters. Don't worry about us, so far you're not close to our positions."

"Bert, I bet he's looking at our tracer burnout and doesn't realize where we're hitting," I said. "Better warn him that our fire is deceptive, if he's depending on the tracers to mark from."

Bert tried to explain to our friend on the ground, but Two Tango still wanted us to move our fire one hundred meters closer to his position. I moved the FLIR crosshairs 25 meters in from the wall and locked on to a point between the adviser's bunker and the one we'd already hit. We fired again.

"Stinger, that's better. Now move it another 50 meters in. That should put it right on."

Delta Two Tango felt that now he was talking us onto the right target. Bert reminded him again about tracer burnout, but he was adamant. I moved the impact point another ten meters. This put it within 30 meters of the friendly bunker. Bert was smoking two cigarettes now. We fired and waited for Two Tango to respond. The response was slow. The background noise was intense with much screaming in Vietnamese.

"Uh, Stinger 36, Delta Two Tango." In the background, the Vietnamese voices were still yelling at full volume. They were more excited than ever. "Uh, Stinger, be advised everybody's all right down here. But, I'd like you to move it out about 70 meters toward the fence."

Now that Delta Two Tango understood that it was easier to give us the target and let us adjust fire than try to guess where our minigun slugs were going, things progressed faster. We raked the walls with miniguns and fired our Vulcans just outside the wire at suspected troop concentrations. The NVA began to retreat from their positions in the compound. The battle was still in progress when we realized that we were going to run out of fuel before we ran out of targets. Bert called Alleycat to send our next gunship up to finish working the TIC. By the time the replacement Stinger entered the area, and we briefed him on the situation, it was time for us to leave. Bert was out of cigarettes.

***

Our squadron sent a total of three airplanes to work with Delta Two Tango during the night. One of our Stingers remained on station over him until past dawn. The last aircraft was able to set up a range and bearing offset in their fire control computer toward where Delta Two Tango believed a communist with a bullhorn was hiding as he tried to convince the South Vietnamese defenders to surrender. After a couple of bursts into the area, the bullhorn was quiet. The NVA attack was beaten back by dawn.

About two weeks after this engagement, an army helicopter pilot passing through Bien Hoa visited our operations shack. He handed our squadron Duty Officer a large cardboard box.

Inside the box was a bullet shredded megaphone, compliments of Delta Two Tango.

***

By the Book Bert was not the only Bien Hoa Stinger with an appropriate nickname. There was another lieutenant I thought of as Bunker Bill. I had met Bill in ROTC summer camp long before either of us was commissioned into the Air Force. We wound up in the same class in Navigation School. Then we got the same gunship class assignment. Bill was a good guy, I thought. He just took everything too seriously. For instance, when Bill decided that no rocket was going to get him, he went all out to make sure he was right. Bill made his bed into a bunker.

He and his roommate were a real Mutt and Jeff pair. Bill was about five foot, eight inches tall and John must have been at least a skinny six foot, six. John's dry sense of humor and not so subtle remarks sometimes antagonized Bill. Bill was a good target for John, but was such a serious person that often he didn't realize when John was joking.

John took the top bunk at Bien Hoa because Bill wanted the lower one, where he could take cover more quickly during rocket attacks. Bill then began to fortify the lower bunk with sand-filled ammo cans. While the rest of us relaxed in the dayroom, Bill perspired in the hot sun, filling and hauling the cans to stack around and above the level of his lower bunk. Above him, John lounged in the top bunk with a paperback and ridiculed his efforts.

Eventually Bill completed his project and invited me down to show it off. The entire bunk was enclosed with the heavy green cans. They were high enough that if Bill was surprised in his bunk, he might be spared shrapnel wounds.

But his real plan, if he had ample warning, was to wriggle under the bed through the one narrow gap he'd left in the armor. Bill demonstrated. He was through the gap in a flash and disappeared into the darkness. When I stooped to look under the bed, all I could see was a beady eye in the shadows. Bill crawled out.

"Larry, they're sending me back to NKP for a couple of weeks," he said. "Your additional duty here is billeting officer. Would you please make sure I get this same room when I come back?"

"Bill, after that much work, I'll make sure no one else but John even comes in here while you're gone. You've earned this hole."

One dark night not long after Bunker Bill headed back to Thailand, six or seven of us were sitting in the dayroom part of our building, watching news on the Armed Forces television channel, AFVN. The announcer was discussing the slow progress the South Vietnamese were making in ousting the NVA from some province, when our warning sirens began to howl. A step behind the sirens, the 122mm rockets began to impact around the base. The ones that struck farther away made a rolling echoing boom. The close ones cracked wickedly, shaking the flimsy walls with concussion. Most of these were close. Ignoring common sense, which dictated hitting the floor and getting as low as possible, every Stinger in the room jumped to his feet and raced down the hall, heading for Bunker Bill's fort.

We were disappointed though, because when we all crowded into the room, shoving and tripping to be first to crawl under Bill's bunk, we found a set of long skinny legs protruding from the narrow entry gap. John had rolled off his bunk, and fallen five feet to the floor, only to find he was too tall to make the sharp entry turn and get under the bed. The scene was enough to make the rest of us forget the rockets.

When Bill returned to claim his castle, John no longer made comments about his bunker.

***

Like Bill, all the Stingers at Bien Hoa were on temporary duty from either NKP or Da Nang. I preferred the flying at Bien Hoa because of the variety of missions. We were assigned everything from base defense to special rescue missions for odd units way out in the boonies.

In Tay Ninh province a solitary conical mountain juts majestically above Tay Ninh city. The mountain is called Nui Ba Den, which supposedly means Black Virgin Mountain. It is not that tall a mountain, but it is the only one around, as if the Black Virgin had wandered off to be by herself. The Americans had built a large communications and control site called Sundog Alpha on top of the mountain.

The bad guys owned the slopes of the mountain, and the good guys lived on top, usually resupplied by helicopter. Until the Easter Invasion, the two groups generally left one another alone, unless one side was trying to prove something to the other. The relationship was ordinarily one of mutual non-interference.

During the Invasion, however, tactical air support was necessary whenever the newcomers, the NVA, took offense to an American detachment perched in the middle of nowhere. Because troops on the sides of the mountain were greatly exposed to defensive fire, usually the NVA would try to knock the Americans off the top only at night or in bad weather.

When we got the call diverting us to Tay Ninh, the bad weather made the night even blacker. Clouds were layered from the ground all the way to B- 52 altitudes. The enemy had chosen a good night for their work and were coming up the hillside in droves. So far no other airplanes had been able to get in to help. If the situation got much worse, the site might have to be abandoned.

As we tried to find clear air between cloud layers, Bert contacted the Sundog Alpha folks for an update on the enemy forces. The major attack was being channeled mainly up known paths to the top, because parts of the mountain were too steep to climb and shoot at the same time.

The big problem was still the weather. The guys on the mountain top said that the bottom of the Black Virgin was socked in and a layer of clouds was hanging just above the mountain.

Eventually, we worked out a plan in which we descended blindly into the clouds on a heading away from the mountain, searching for that magic layer of cloud-free air that would let us come to the mountain in the clear. It was difficult to tell in the blackness when we were in a clear patch. When it looked as good as it was going to get, we headed toward the Black Virgin. We hoped our altimeter settings were accurate enough to keep us from plowing into the side of the hill.

We asked Sundog Alpha to put up a few flares as we headed in. When we got closer, we could see the flares and sure enough, we were in between cloud layers and just above the mountain. The Sundog crowd helped direct our fire on the paths the enemy were using and kept flares up to help us see the mountain.

Because the top of the hill was so small, and because the enemy was only on certain sides, we decided the best tactic was simply to fly around the top of the mountain and let the pilot fire manually when we came abreast of the bad guys. This worked well as long as flares were illuminating the mountain. The pilot rocked the wings as we fired, and the moving red streams walked the mountain, sending ricochets up and down the slopes. When we were pretty sure the attack was broken, we climbed out through the clouds and headed home.

The next day we received a message of thanks and the word that 75 blood trails had been found on the mountain's sides. The best thing for me about the mission was that Bert had switched to a pipe, and I hadn't been blinded by clouds of smoke as we let down through the weather.

Sometimes we were disappointed and surprised with the way our Bien Hoa missions ended. In Tay Ninh, there was a huge rectangular monastery complex. Long walls surrounded buildings and shrines. We were called into the area to help South Vietnamese forces which had taken defensive positions in and around the monastery. It was virtually the only real estate left in friendly hands in Tay Ninh.

Our gunship spent about three hours over that monastery, dropping flares and firing at NVA positions in and around it, and when we left all was quiet. The enemy forces had broken off their attack and the area was in friendly hands.

All the way back to Bien Hoa, we congratulated ourselves as saviors for the South Vietnamese garrison. We debriefed with the intelligence folks and when we went to bed early that morning, we were convinced that the defenders would probably recommend us for decorations.

When we were up and about later in the morning, I turned on the television to check the news. The channel's hottest news was that the city had fallen, early in the morning. The bad guys had waited us out, and attacked when we were long gone.

***

The fall season was passing unnoticed in South Vietnam. The news was full of shuttle diplomacy, secret peace talks and American air strikes against the North. Our war had settled into a routine, flying every other night against targets in the local area. We were doing our own shuttling as well, from Bien Hoa to Da Nang. We usually flew a mission out of Bien Hoa and recovered at Da Nang to drop off those crewmembers who were remaining there. Although I preferred Bien Hoa, it was my turn to visit our Da Nang home.

Our enroute mission was to check out boat traffic on the Mekong in southern Cambodia. The first step was to boresight our guns. To accomplish this, we had to find some clear spot where we could see the flash of the 20mm shells' impact. On the edge of the river, near where another river joined the main stream, we found what we were looking for, and fired the first marking burst.

"Good Lord, Bert!" I shouted. "Look at that."

A flotilla of sampans was shoving off from the bank. Some looked like big yachts. The hot spots on some indicated motorized boats, while others appeared to be the smaller type, driven by long sweeps. They were rapidly scattering up and down the river.

"Looks like cockroaches when you turn on the light," Bert replied. "Looks like we've run into a supply depot area."

We rolled into orbit above the largest boat, which was making good time upstream. The NOS said he could see a white bow wave marking the Mekong's dark waters. In moments we were set up to fire. Leading the boat with the FLIR crosshairs, I waited.

"I wish we'd had time to tweak the guns," said the pilot. "Into the sight, FLIR. Corning to you."

The one Vulcan cannon and two miniguns we had on line roared in the cargo compartment, but I saw no flashes on target in the FLIR screen. The cannon shells were impacting somewhere in the water but we couldn't tell where. They weren't exploding on the water's surface and without tweaking in our fire computer, we didn't know how far off the aim point our shells were hitting. All we could do was keep firing.

Two bursts later, the big boat began to slow down. Something odd was happening to it in my FLIR screen.

Its image was growing fainter, as if it were fading out. Before our eyes, the boat disappeared from the screen.

"It's crossover," Bert said, pointing at my screen.

"I don't think so, Bert. I can still see other boats." There is a phenomenon associated with infra-red sensors called crossover. Since different objects warmed and cooled at different rates during the day, the temperature differential between objects allowed us to see them on the screen. A bridge over a stream, for instance, would show up because the water and the bridge had different temperature levels. But when the bridge cooled in

140

the evening, it might temporarily match the temperature of the water below. That was crossover, and the bridge would disappear from the screen as it blended with the water.

"The boat just sank, you guys," the NOS yelled from below. "Don't you want to get on some other targets?" We chased boats for half an hour; until all the survivors were so well hidden we couldn't pick them out of the trees overhanging the river bank. Then we moved back to the point where we had first surprised them and fired at suspicious looking spots. We hoped to hit paydirt with a lucky burst into a supply cache. We started some small fires, but were disappointed that no big secondary explosions came up.

We regretted having to leave before we could really do a good job on the area, but we had to go all the way to Da Nang. We called in the target location and turned north. Airstrikes were would be diverted into the area after we departed.

Landing at Da Nang was nothing out of the ordinary, until we stopped on the taxiway to do our ordinary after landing engine runup for maintenance. I sat drowsily in the "jumpseat" that folded down from a wall bracket beside the bulletproof curtain and listened to the pilots and flight engineer go through their checklists.

Suddenly loud pops were audible over the noise of the racing recip engine on the right wing. Backfire, I thought and leaned forward to see the engine. I saw instead a sudden black fountain of dirt burst into the air from the grassy area just in front of our nose.

"Rockets!" I keyed the mike, and standing, slammed the jumpseat into its bracket. Turning and reaching to disconnect my interphone cord, I jumped down to the big box we used as a step between the cargo compartment and cockpit and sprinted toward the rear of the plane. Sitting in an airplane on the ground, surrounded by fuel and explosives, was not the place to be during an artillery attack and we all knew it.

The rest of the crew was moving quickly too. By the time I reached the rear exit hatch, the grass beside the taxiway held five horizontal figures, side by side, each trying to squirm flatter in the dirt. They looked like five pigs lined up for supper against an invisible sow.

As I leaped from the airplane to join them, a rocket slammed into a rescue helicopter in the closest revetment, breaking it into fiery halves and spraying shrapnel above the revetment walls. I landed, skidding, on the grass next to the other five guys already there. Behind me, the rest of the crew was thundering out of the plane.

I felt something, a lump, soft and sticky, against my belly. I wondered if the shrapnel from that last rocket had got me. I rolled over on my side and looked down. Relief flooded over me. Instead of bloodstains, there were only the remains of the giant, smelly puff-ball mushroom I'd crushed in my headlong dive to the ground. The fungus seemed to be my personal welcome back to Da Nang.

WINDING DOWN

This short stay at Da Nang was memorable for a single occurrence. They sent me back to NKP to close down the squadron there and move it to Da Nang. My official squadron additional duties included being the assistant supply officer. This meant little to me, for most of the time I was not around our parent squadron in Thailand to worry about such things. Occasionally, however, I would be captured while passing through NKP, and be forced to attend one of the many supply and budget meetings. Each time this occurred, I simply sat back in the upholstered chair and nodded my head as if I understood perfectly well what we were talking about. After all, we had a real supply and budget guy to do what was necessary.

As our leaders realized the NVA's invasion had been thwarted, plans were made to deliver more military hardware to our allies in the South. Part of this gear would ultimately include our AC-119K gunships. To prepare for the transfer of aircraft, we had to get them all to Vietnam. We were closing down the Stingers in NKP.

Unfortunately our supply guy was not in Southeast Asia at all. He was on leave somewhere in Hawaii.

I would have to handle it. "No trick for a show dog," Walt said.

When I arrived at NKP, I was shown the paperwork I needed to complete. Most of our equipment and the maintenance gear associated with the airplanes would be going to Vietnam with them, so I wouldn't have to worry about that. My problem was to find all the real property the base said we owned and to mark it for turn-in. This property was more than just the buildings our people lived in; it consisted of fans, refrigerators, chairs, tables and other portable items. In a casual environment like NKP, with a war going on, and when people didn't hang around longer than one year, property turnover was amazing.

I took our inventory list and did a solo preparatory walk through of our area and buildings. There were loads of items like the ones on my list, but the serial numbers didn't match. Somewhere along the line, much of our stuff had been borrowed or stolen, or more likely, broken. Still, I had to turn in the right amount and kinds of furniture.

So I did the only thing I could; I visited our squadron First Sergeant and together we made a plan. The next morning, I was out early with my list. With me, I had four of the biggest, ugliest, meanest looking senior gunners in our squadron. Together, we scoured the base, going from hootch to hootch. I read the items from the list and the gunners looked for the item or a suitable replacement.

"One each metal lawn chair, green," I read. "That looks like our lawn chair," said a gunner, pointing to a brown chair.

"Right. That's it, all right," said another.

"Get your ass outta our chair," said the biggest gunner, and then the last guy would pick up the furniture and take it to our van.

The gunners took turns doing their favorite part, which was saying, "Get your ass outta our chair," or "offa our table," or whatever. Our inventory was done in a jiffy. The only hard part was finding the original owners of the stuff we actually had, but weren't authorized.

With the real property all accounted for, I signed the inventory sheet and jumped on a plane back to Da Nang before anyone could ask questions. I wasn't worried. After all, what could they do, send me to Vietnam?

Back at Da Nang, virtually all our missions were flown into the rocket belt around the base. The army helicopters had caught some of the enemy setting up rockets, and they called in our aircraft. The gunships destroyed the rockets and killed many of the rocketeers. The South Vietnamese captured other wounded persons after the gunships had finished.

The Stars and Stripes ran an article about the action. The bad guys had forcibly conscripted village women and young girls to carry the rockets to their planned launching point. The rain of fire from the sky and the exploding rockets were terrifying for one young girl that reporters interviewed in the hospital. She and her mother had not wanted to help with the rockets, she said, but when the enemy came with guns and made them carry rockets, what could they do?

The helicopter pilots who worked out of Marble Mountain into the rocket belt were good at their mission. They ran the mission with two helicopters, a low bird and a high one. The high bird kept flares in the air while the low one poked around bunkers and jungle with a bright spotlight. They were looking for persons setting up rockets or mortars.

Before our gunships began to work with helicopters, the bad guys would often fire on the choppers and then retreat into bunkers. The helicopters' armament couldn't touch them and choppers were being hit hard with the enemy's heavy machineguns. With the new Army-Air Force cooperation process, the helicopters would mark the bunkers with white phosphorous rockets. Then the Air Force gunships would move in and use the Vulcans to reduce the target. Then the helicopters would come in for a BDA. These damage assessments were often explicitly gory. The chopper pilots seemed to take pleasure in adding up the arms and legs and dividing by two to see how many persons had been in the bunker.

145

We would monitor the helicopter frequency to be ready in case they needed us. The radio exchanges between the helicopter pilots and their command post expressed, better than any reporter ever could, the attitude created by constant exposure to danger and violence.

"Command post, this is Two Two. We got a guy down here in black pajamas with a basket. He's hiding behind some trees. What do you want us to do?" The helicopter pilot's voice vibrated with the engine roar. It was well after midnight and the choppers' bright light was pointed at the side of an abandoned bunker.

"It's too early to be going to market; grease him," their command post replied.

Machinegun tracers licked out from the hovering helicopter in a long burst and then the helicopter moved casually away.

I was glad to fly as few missions as possible from Da Nang and get back to Bien Hoa where I hoped there would be more variety in our missions.

* * *

I could feel my tension grow as we realized the war would soon halt for the Americans. Massive B-52 bombing raids over North Vietnam and the NVA losses in the Easter Offensive had brought the North Vietnamese to the negotiating table. But it was the Americans, not the South Vietnamese, who were doing the negotiation, and we all knew that war protests at home would play a big part in determining how hard we bargained. The settlement would be in America's best interests, not necessarily our allies'.

I didn't want to make any mistakes this close to the end. Our missions from Bien Hoa began to feel like those from Da Nang.

We put in a lot of time going in circles over Saigon, in the hopes that our presence would deter rocket attacks.

For me, the war's end was more of a let-down than a climax. There was no last great battle. I flew the next to last gunship sortie of the war from Bien Hoa, when we were sent out to an empty rice paddy area we had hit many times before. There were no targets there, but we were directed to put tracers and cannon shells into the mud. It was a waste of ammunition. When we landed after midnight, the war was over for me.

HOMEWARD BOUND

At noon the following day, as I walked up the hill to my room from lunch, I stopped beside the street to let a Vietnamese soldier zoom by on a whining motorbike. One unflattering nickname sometimes assigned for these soldiers was Zips. I was told the name derived from the way they fatalistically zipped through intersections on their bikes without heed of traffic signs or traffic. Zip seemed an appropriate title for the bike riders of Bien Hoa.

I watched the Vietnamese as he sped down the hill toward an intersection. In the barracks by the crossroads, a few Marines sat on the steps in the sun. True to form, the biker ran the stop sign just as a jeep entered the intersection. The bike hit the right front jeep tire and fell down.

The whining engine was silenced by the impact. The rider continued on, tumbling over the jeep's hood and rolling into the dust on the other side. The jeep driver looked at the bike on one side, at the rider on the other, and then drove on through the intersection and down the hill.

Three Marines rose from the steps and walked to the Vietnamese. Two Marines, one black and the other white, picked the small soldier up by each arm, and with their hats, dusted him off. The third Marine righted the bike, looked at the damaged front wheel, then kick-started the engine.

They hoisted the dazed soldier onto the seat, made sure he had a firm grip on the handlebars, and gave him a push to start him down the street. The Vietnamese, front wheel wobbling, weaved down the hill, like a cartoon character come to life. The three Marines, with solemn faces, returned to the steps. They never smiled during the whole operation. It was as if they had been waiting for a regularly scheduled event, like a train. They had caught the 12 o'clock Zip.

I collapsed into the grass, tears of laughter rolling down my face. It felt good to laugh; the grass smelled good and the tears carried away the tension.

***

Walt and I were at the boarding ramp early. The Da Nang air terminal area looked like a cattle shipping dock. Small roofed areas provided shelter from the sun. White fences stretched everywhere to ensure that people stayed in line. We were going home, as soon as they opened up the "Freedom Bird" that sat waiting for us on the parking ramp.

Walt and I were determined to get good seats this trip. We had been waiting for two hours and were at the very front of the line. A skinny paper pusher walked to the front of the boarding steps with a microphone. "All right, folks," he said. "We're going to board the airplane by rank. All colonels, lieutenant colonels and majors to the front, please. Remember, RHIP."

I looked at Walt and shook my head. It didn't matter to me. Any seat home would be a good one.

THE END

PHOTOS

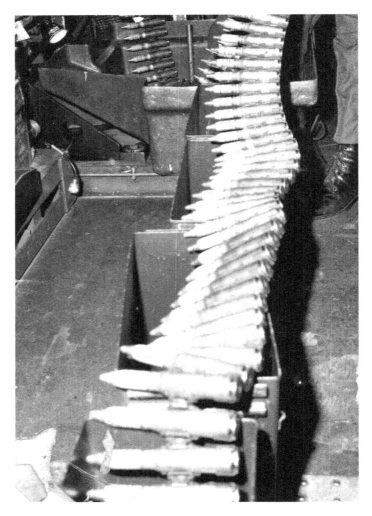

20 mm ammunition for the Vulcan cannons.

Gunners setting up guns. Note survival vests, parachute harness for chest pack chute, interphone cord and 38 caliber revolver on nearest gunner. Even while airborne the aircrew was heavily laden.

Left to right: Lt. Col. Taschiologlou, Lt. Barbee, and SSgt. Bare after rescue by helicopter, headed into the hospital for a checkup. The multiple white cords on the survival vests secure individual pieces of equipment to the vest.

Survivors of the shoot down with the aircraft that led the rescue mission. The Proud American had a Medal of Honor history. A pilot flying this particular A-1E Skyraider had been awarded the medal for a mission when flying it.

Lt. Barbee at the Night Observation Sight (NOS) position.
Courtesy of Frank Baehre.

Lt. Barbee at NKP. These comfortable old flight suits
were the customary non-mission attire while on base.

Debbie and Larry in a borrowed trailer at NKP. More senior officers often were billeted 2 to a trailer.

Debbie and Larry prior to military retirement in 1990.

AFTERWARD

Walt and I boarded the Freedom Bird from Vietnam more than 45 years ago. Nearly 20 years after that departure, I wrote this story as my project for a masters' degree in journalism from the University of Oklahoma. Typically for me, I had waited until the deadline was approaching and then decided I'd better write about something I knew.

My son helped set up my office with my easy chair, my steam-driven, double-drive, floppy-disk computer, dot-matrix printer, and a stereo headset over which I repeatedly played the movie sound tracks of "Gettysburg" and "Forest Gump," and also the album "In-Country—Folk Songs of Americans in the Vietnam War." I still recommend the "Gettysburg" soundtrack for serious thinking music.

The music seemed to help bring back memories and set the mood for scenes. In seven non-stop days I completed the story and submitted it to the graduate committee. Then I put the story in a box in the garage, stuffed the memories in with it, and closed the lid on it all.

Over the years, when friends learned I had a "story," they asked if they could read it, so I dug it out, made a copy for them and took pains to forget it again. I learned that when you take memories out of a box, sometimes it takes a while to put them all away again.

Somewhere along the line the story arrived on our AC-119 Gunship Association's website. Colonel Roy Davis read the story and suggested that it might be interesting and useful for our organization if it were available in an individual format.

I hope you found something worth your while in the reading. LDB 2019.

ABOUT THE AUTHOR

Larry Barbee was born in rural north Texas. He received his BS degree from Texas A&M University in January, 1970 and was commissioned into the Air Force the same day. He and the former Deborah Grider were married in September, 1970.

He graduated from Air Force Undergraduate Navigator Training at Mather AFB, CA, in 1971 and was assigned to the 18th Special Operations Squadron to fly AC-119K "Stinger" gunships in Southeast Asia. In 1972-73 he accumulated more than 140 missions and 400 combat flying hours over Laos, South Vietnam and Cambodia.

Upon return to the United States Lt. Barbee was assigned to Mather AFB as an Instructor Navigator in the T-29C and the T-43A aircraft. In 1976 the Barbees were reassigned to F-111F fighter-bombers in Idaho, and subsequently, England. Captain Barbee served as squadron Executive Officer, Wing Plans Officer, Instructor Weapon System Officer in the Wing's Replacement Training Unit, and squadron Flight Commander.

In 1981 Larry and Debbie returned to Keesler AFB, MS where Larry served as a Battlestaff Operations Officer, Director of Airborne Battlestaff, and Asst. Chief of Concepts and Tactics for the 7th Airborne Battlefield Command, Control and Communications (ABCCC) Squadron.

He participated in Operation Urgent Fury in Grenada to protect American civilians and return control of the Grenadian government to its rightful officials after a coup by pro-communist leaders. He accumulated combat support flying hours in the EC-130 during the invasion and follow-on operations.

In 1984 Larry was assigned to the Operations Section of the 28th Air Division at Tinker AFB, Oklahoma. He served as Chief, EC-130

Operations and Asst. Chief, Division Current Operations. He was also the Air Division's primary point of contact with the Special Operations community. While at Tinker he received his MA from the University of Oklahoma.

Major Barbee retired from active duty in 1990. For the next 28 years he worked as a safety professional in the insurance industry and is now retired. Larry and Debbie live near Austin, Texas where Debbie has developed her skills and business as a jewelry artist. They have three children, one each born in California, Idaho and England.

Made in the USA
Monee, IL
09 December 2019

18235036R00089